mediterranean
recipes
to enjoy with friends

polly baptist

foulsham
LONDON • NEW YORK • TORONTO • SYDNEY

foulsham

The Publishing House, Bennetts Close, Cippenham,
Slough, Berkshire, SL1 5AP, England

Thanks to my editor, Wendy Hobson, and the team at Foulsham for making this book possible.
Thanks also to all the yacht owners and their guests who I have cooked for onboard over all the years
and for encouraging me to write a book, but most of all to my parents who instilled in me a love of
food and cooking whilst I grew up and continue to do so and also to Mike for his help and support
whilst we continue to work together at sea onboard these luxury yachts.

ISBN 0-572-03050-9

Photographs by Carol and Terry Pastor

Cover photographs by Alexis Andrews

A CIP record for this book is available from the British Library

Printed in Great Britain by St Edmundsbury Press, Bury St Edmunds, Suffolk

Contents

From My Galley to Your Kitchen

I have been working as a chef on board luxury yachts, mainly sailing boats, for more than 14 years. My first onboard job – supposedly a temporary one – was a six-month summer assignment in Greece and Turkey, with the idea of then returning to California where I was working as a fashion designer, having graduated in fashion design from university. I have yet to return to the industry! One season ran into another, and since it's always summer somewhere and the yachts follow the summer season, I continued working on different yachts as I enjoyed the work and loved to cook. I completed a cookery course, to give me more confidence and teach me some tricks of the trade, and I continue to learn more all the time from working on different boats, cooking for various owners or charter guests, and spending time in kitchens ashore whenever I can.

I work as a member of a crew on five-star yachts sailing around the world. We give the most individual service possible and a first-class one at that. There are rules and regulations that we all have to abide by – as in any industry – and we have to gain proper qualifications if we wish to become skippers, engineers, chefs, or whatever.

If you imagine that we just lie out in the sun all day and enjoy ourselves cruising around the world, then think again. There are relaxing moments, of course, and the times we can take it easy are when we do ocean crossings, for example from the Mediterranean to the Caribbean or to the Seychelles. Then we get the time to read a book on the foredeck and enjoy a small portion of what others pay for. But for Mediterranean cruises when guests are on board – and that can be for months at a time – our days are long, usually lasting from about 6 am until midnight. We provide a service for the owners and their guests to ensure that they can relax and enjoy their holidays on board. It's a 24/7 365 days a year job, meaning that we are on call 24 hours a day, 7 days a week, 365 days a year. It's really full time.

The pressure is as intense as in any restaurant I have worked in – if not more so. I am the only person in the galley in charge of the food and drinks, so there is no one else to blame or fall back on should something go wrong. I'm on call all the time; there's nowhere to escape and my shift never ends. The workplace can be dangerous and difficult to cope with, too. It's not quite as bad if the cooker is fitted with a gimbal – a device that keeps it more or less level while the boat is moving. But you can imagine that, without one, some dishes can be near-on catastrophes and just opening a fridge door at the wrong moment can lead to a real mess. Sailing yachts are a particular problem as the boats are often heeling over and the storage areas are seriously compact.

All these things make it a challenge but it's one I love and thrive on. For this reason, I decided to write this book, to give others some insight into what it is like to work as a chef on board a private luxury yacht. So I collected together some of my favourite recipes, with a few anecdotes about cruising the Mediterranean. If you have been lucky enough to spend a holiday this way, you'll find that the flavours and dishes I've chosen will bring back the most wonderful memories. Even if you haven't, they'll still taste pretty wonderful!

What's more, the style of cooking that I use on board is perfect for busy modern cooks. I choose dishes that are light and healthy and easy to prepare; they must use the best-quality, fresh ingredients; they have to look vibrant, colourful and enticing, and taste as good as anything you'll find in a five-star restaurant – because that's what my employers and their guests expect. Most of the celebrities I have cooked for certainly wouldn't put up with anything less.

So, in the comfort – if not the sunshine – of your own home, with the added benefits of plenty of storage space and a kitchen that stays in one place, you can enjoy this mouth-watering selection of just some of the recipes that have been tried and tested on my voyages. While many have their origins in the Mediterranean, you'll find that I take inspiration from anywhere and everywhere, so there are plenty of flavours to enjoy from around the world. I hope you enjoy them as much as I do.

An Italian Cruise

It was late March when my partner, Mike, and I flew up to Italy, arriving tanned from a long summer in Australia to start our contract on board a brand new boat. We were greeted by the skipper, Noel, at Pisa airport, and driven past the famous Leaning Tower on route to Viareggio, where the boat was in the latter stages of construction. After a warm Australian summer our arrival in a chilly spring, where the snow was still on the mountains high above the town, was a bit of a shock.

The boat we joined was a 30-metre motor yacht constructed by Falcon Yachts. The owner, Gary, liked to cruise around the Mediterranean during the summer months, while his home base in Auckland, New Zealand was in the midst of winter. On our arrival, the vessel, which was soon to be christened *QED (Quod Erat Demonstrandum)* had been floating for just 14 days and had not yet ventured out of the port as there was still so much to do.

The most important area to me was the galley – that's always the first place I check out. This one was well laid out except for the fact that there was a washing machine and dryer at one end. This used up valuable space and made the galley extremely hot when the dryer was running, despite the fully ducted air-conditioning. However, the space worked well and it proved to be a galley I enjoyed cooking in. All the appliances were high quality, and the electric oven and hob were so shiny and new I was worried to use them to start with – but I soon got over that! Everything on board these vessels – whether in the galley, engine room, saloon or anywhere else – is always kept in the most immaculate as-new condition, despite the amount of hard wear it gets. As well as the hob and oven, washer and dryer, this galley also had the essential dishwasher, two fridges and a freezer, which we always kept full. With hindsight, bigger fridges would have been useful, but I have always managed with what I have. The worktop was marble – great to work on, easy to keep hygienically clean, and cool to the touch regardless of the temperature outside and the working dishwasher beneath.

QED also had her own air-conditioned wine cellar, where we decided we had room to place another large fridge for drinks, so I ordered that to be delivered – hoping it would arrive before we left port. This idea had come up during our discussions with Gary when he admitted to the amount of beer he and his guests tended to consume. I could easily see that as the vessel only had two small bar fridges, which were clearly not going to be up to the consumption rate of these thirsty Kiwis, an extra fridge was going to be crucial to the happiness of all onboard! However, I decided that the two ice-makers should be up to their job.

Planning ahead

When you are responsible for feeding about 30 different guests with varying appetites for a 12-week cruise, you need to do quite a bit of advance planning. The first stage is to talk to the owner and find out as much as you can about him and his guests for the cruise, their likes, dislikes and dietary habits.

This time, I was excited to learn that I had an open invitation to cook a variety of menus. The food style was to be health-conscious, light, fresh and full of flavour. The onboard style was generally informal, with the occasional, no-boundaries formal dinner. So I collected together some of my favourite and most successful recipes in a variety of styles, which I thought were bound to impress.

I also began to list the foods I would need to buy in advance, and the fresh ingredients I would have to buy each time we moored. It is hard to judge quantities required for the length of the cruise and the number of guests, plus the crew, of course. Some people eat much more than you expect and others far less! However, I have quite a lot of experience of working it out now and, at the end of the season, I usually find my forecasts have been pretty accurate. Cooking three times a day for at least 12 hungry mouths means a lot of food! As well as all the non-perishable items that I take on board, I knew we would have to shop for huge amounts of food virtually every day. I filled the two fridges to bursting every morning, though by the next day they would be fairly empty. Just to give you an idea of the quantities, the guests and crew went through ten yoghurts, 2 litres of milk and copious amounts of fresh fruit and fresh juices at every breakfast; this amount of food alone left quite a gap in our previously well-stocked fridge. So throughout the season, I performed a juggling act to make sure we had enough of everything.

Stocking the galley

When stocking a galley, I try to buy enough dried food for most of the season, as long as I can fit it into the storage spaces available. This makes life much easier once you get on board as you don't have to worry about the basics, such as sugar, flour and so on.

I also need to stock up on anything I can't buy in the ports we visit. The food that is now available throughout the Mediterranean region has improved tenfold since the early 1990s, making things much easier. At that time it was extremely difficult to get anything other than the local produce. For example, in Greece, you could only buy Greek cheeses like Feta, Halloumi and Mezithra, and there was nowhere you could buy Indian spices in Italy. So with that in mind, I went on a shopping trip in London before I boarded the boat to pick up some of the things I thought might be difficult to buy in the Med. In particular, I bought preserves, plus Chinese, Thai and Indian spices and condiments that I knew I would use during the season and had them sent down to the boat.

I also like to make my own preserves and condiments to take on board so, as early as I could, I started making chilli oils, herb oils, coloured oils, plus jams (conserves) and chutneys that I would use throughout the season. These play an important part in my daily menus, whether they are served at breakfast or lunch or used to garnish the plates. Sometimes, I have time during a trip to make preserves with fresh produce bought in ports we visit, which is always well received by the guests as they eat their fresh rolls or home-baked bread with home-made jams and preserves.

To stock the wine cellar, we took delivery of two large orders of wine from France during the cruise, and by the end of the summer we had very little left. Luckily for us, this wine cellar – like many on board larger yachts now – was a sophisticated affair, as the owner understood how wines can suffer from the motion of the boat. Many yachts do two trans-Atlantic crossings a year, which damage the wines as the waves roll the bottles around for three weeks each crossing! Wines should really be kept at a constant temperature of around 22°C (71°F) – which we tried to keep with our air-conditioning – and it is recommended that they remain upright, rather than on their sides. So with our wine cellar and the large bar fridge, there was not going to be a problem with cold drinks onboard this boat!

If all else fails, you can always get in touch with supply agents who send out provision lists of foods and wines that they can deliver to the yacht wherever it is, or they can provision the yacht for you if you have a particularly hectic schedule. Not surprisingly, this comes at a price. But they are very useful for stocking up, especially when you are chartering as there is very little time between one job and the next, so using the agents to help you out can make life much easier.

Storing the food

On a yacht, every inch of storage space is filled to the brim. The galley on this motor yacht had small cupboards, which meant a limited amount of room. I filled this quickly so that everything I needed was within arm's reach, such as my herbs and spices, flours, sugars and so on. Most of the fresh food was stored in the fridges. The onions, potatoes, garlic and lemons lived in baskets in the galley. But it didn't stop there. There was always a large bowl of fruit in the saloon as it was consumed at such a rapid rate – I simply topped it up from the galley. In addition, food was kept in the seat of the bridge, under the stairs, in the wine cellar, under the seat in the galley, in the locker by the crew companionway and in the bilge in the crew quarters. And, apart from the wine cellar, we had drinks in the many seat lockers and deck lockers on the fly bridge.

Local supplies

As I mentioned, when we're cruising we have to shop regularly for fresh food, and at times Mike felt as though he had been demoted from first mate to bag mule!

Bread was fresh every day, brought by the guests or Mike when they went ashore in the mornings for a walk and to find the papers. I do bake bread regularly, often putting unbaked dough in the freezer for baking later, but with the variety of fresh breads available in Italy it is almost crazy to bake it yourself. I also had some part-baked loaves in the freezer as a back-up, and they came in handy from time to time.

The Italian delis and markets are amongst my favourites in the Mediterranean region. The delis are always so full of fantastic meats, cheeses, vegetables, marinated fish, oils and, of course, pasta. It is easy to see why the Italian cuisine has been adopted with such gusto by so many countries. For me, the delis were always a place to stop and look for inspiration for the next meals. In the early stages of this cruise, my Italian was quite poor and we had some hilarious experiences when my Italian failed me as I tried to communicate the required quantities of foods such as prosciutto, olives or sun-dried tomatoes. However, the Italians are wonderful people and really eager to help you even if your Italian isn't up to much.

Markets everywhere around the Mediterranean are renowned for being wonderful, offering the best-quality fresh produce, but for me there are not many places that can beat those in Italy. They are always situated in the centre of the towns, generally in buildings that have been designed specifically to hold the stalls, and they often have butchers, bakeries and delis around the sides of the building. They are based on the ancient Roman and Greek style of market. The market in Florence is one that everyone should visit, given the chance, even if you are not buying food, as it is one of the best and the town itself is magnificent too. Having said that, there are dozens of others that I could list as worth seeing, but you can be sure that my list would never end as I am always finding new markets in new places that become significant to my visit.

Viareggio's market was small but always full of good fresh produce that sold out quickly at the start of the day. By the marina where we were moored, there was a canal on which they held a daily fish market, where the stallholders sold their fresh fish from the sides of the boats under the shade of umbrellas when the summer sun became too hot. They mainly sold small fish suitable for frying (sautéing) or using in fish soups: calamari, scampi and whitebait, to name just a few. The fish were arranged in ice-boxes ready to be snapped up by locals.

I think an integral part of travelling in Italy – or in any country for that matter – is visiting the local delis and markets to experience the wonders of Italian food and the friendliness of the people. You can learn so much about the foods they eat and how to cook items you may not have seen before by asking the locals; it gives you a real feeling for the character of the people and their lives. Some of the best times for me while travelling have been visiting the markets, as it has become a great learning experience. And that's one of the experiences I will try to communicate to you through my recipes and anecdotes in this book.

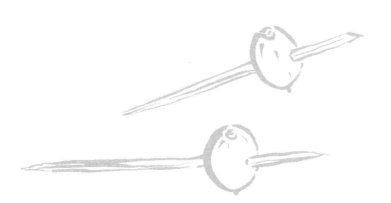

Notes on the Recipes

- The recipes serve 6–8 people unless marked otherwise. Everyone has their own ideas of what makes a portion – mine tend to be fairly generous as fresh air and exercise gives us such an appetite. However, you'll find the recipes easy to scale down if you are cooking for smaller numbers, or you find the servings generous.

- Using scales on a moving vessel can be quite tricky, especially if we are on a heel on a sailing yacht. The best scales I have used at sea are the electronic ones but even they struggle in a rough sea, so I tend to use cups and spoons, having converted a lot of my recipes to this method whilst I am at sea. You'll therefore find cup measures throughout the recipes; as well as the usual metric and imperial equivalents for those of you who prefer the traditional weights.

- Do not mix metric, imperial and American measures. Follow one set only.

- American terms are given in brackets.

- All spoon measurements are level:
1 tsp = 15 ml; 1 tbsp = 15 ml.

- Eggs are medium unless otherwise stated. If you use a different size, adjust the amount of liquid added to obtain the right consistency.

- Always wash, peel, core and seed, if necessary, fresh produce before use. Ensure that all fruit and vegetables are as fresh as possible and in good condition.

- Seasoning and the use of strongly flavoured ingredients, such as onions and garlic, are very much a matter of personal taste. Taste the food as you cook and adjust seasonings to suit your own taste.

- Always use fresh herbs unless dried are specifically called for. If it is necessary to use dried herbs, use half the quantity stated. Chopped frozen varieties are much better than dried. There is no substitute for fresh parsley and coriander (cilantro). I always chop the herbs before I measure the quantity.

- Can and packet sizes are approximate and will depend on the particular brand.

- Use butter or a margarine of your choice in the recipes. Since some margarines or spreads are not suitable for cooking, check the packet before using for the first time.

- Use whichever kitchen gadgets you like to speed up preparation and cooking times: mixers for whisking; food processors for grating, slicing, mixing or kneading; blenders for liquidising.

- All ovens vary, so cooking times have to be approximate. Adjust cooking times and temperatures according to manufacturer's instructions.

- Always preheat a conventional oven and cook on the centre shelf unless otherwise specified. Fan ovens do not require preheating.

starters
and snacks

I always serve starters at dinner but rarely at lunchtime, as everyone cuts down on eating time during the day on the yachts. Serving snacks or canapés at cocktail hour is essential, though, and many of these starters make perfect canapés if you make miniature versions. Becoming adaptable in your cooking ideas gives you endless opportunities to experiment, not just with size but also with style and flavours, and if you try out your own ideas it will give you much more confidence in your cooking.

Fresh hummus

*You can, of course, buy hummus in the supermarket but many brands include
mayonnaise or other extra ingredients. Freshly made hummus has a much deeper
flavour and more texture and makes a great dip to serve with crusty bread or flat breads.*

SERVES 6–8

**300 g/11 oz dried chick peas
(garbanzos)**

150 ml/¼ pt/⅔ cup olive oil

Juice of 3 lemons

15 ml/1 tbsp tahini paste

2 garlic cloves

5 ml/1 tsp ground coriander (cilantro)

Salt and freshly ground black pepper

10 ml/2 tsp ground cumin

1 Soak the chick peas overnight in cold water, then drain and rinse.

2 Place them in a large saucepan and cover with fresh cold water.
Bring to the boil, then simmer for 40 minutes until soft, lifting off the
scum that forms on the top. Top up with boiling water during
cooking, if necessary, to make sure the chick peas remain covered,
otherwise they will not soften.

3 Remove from the heat and drain, reserving the liquid.

4 Blend half the chick peas in a food processor with half the olive oil,
half the lemon juice and 30 ml/2 tbsp of the cooking liquid. Add half
the tahini paste, one garlic clove and half the coriander, blending as
you do this and seasoning to taste with salt and pepper. Repeat with
another 30 ml/2 tbsp of the cooking liquid and all the remaining
ingredients including the cumin. Mix the two batches together, taste
and season again if necessary.

Serving suggestions You can serve this with my Focaccia (see page
138) or any ready-made breads or flat breads.

Hint and variations If you don't have time to cook your own pulses,
just substitute drained canned chick peas for the cooked peas.
100 g/4 oz/⅔ cup of dried chick peas cooks up to be equivalent to
one 425 g/15 oz/large can.

To make this into a salad, mash half the chick peas and leave the
rest whole, then add a few chopped spring onions (scallions),
tomatoes and plenty of chopped fresh parsley or coriander.

Mediterranean flavour This dish originally comes from Crete and was
rarely seen in the eastern Mediterranean.

Tzatziki

A traditional Greek starter – and I learned the traditional way of making it while I was working in Greece. It is obviously made with Greek yoghurt, which is a thick, full-fat yoghurt that is great to use in cooking.

SERVES 6–8

1 large cucumber

Salt

500 ml/17 fl oz/2¼ cups Greek or plain yoghurt

15 ml/1 tbsp olive oil

1 garlic clove, crushed

Freshly ground black pepper

25 g/1 oz/½ cup chopped fresh mint

1 Grate the cucumber, place in a colander and sprinkle generously with salt. Leave to drain for 30 minutes.

2 Squeeze out all the liquid and set the cucumber aside.

3 Place the yoghurt in a bowl and beat in the olive oil and garlic. Season to taste with pepper, then stir in the cucumber and mint.

4 Chill until ready to serve.

Serving suggestions Tzatziki is usually served with thick bread and tastes great with my Focaccia (see page 138).

Hints and variations If you don't have thick Greek yoghurt, you can use a thinner variety, but you need to thicken it before you start. Line a sieve (strainer) with muslin (cheesecloth) or two thicknesses of kitchen paper (paper towels) and pour in the yoghurt. Allow to drain for at least an hour, stirring regularly so that most of the extra water drains off.

Aubergine dip

If you can cook the aubergines over a barbecue, it gives the dish a lovely smoky flavour. I leave some aubergines on the coals as they are dying. However, it is still a great dish if you roast them.

SERVES 6–8

2 medium aubergines (eggplants)

4 garlic cloves, cut into slivers

150 g/5 oz Feta cheese, in a slab

30 ml/2 tbsp olive oil

1 sprig of fresh thyme

Salt and freshly ground black pepper

50 g/2 oz/1 cup chopped fresh parsley

1 Preheat the oven to 200°C/400°F/gas 6/fan oven 180°C.

2 Pierce the aubergines in several places with a sharp knife, then push the slivers of garlic into the slits. Place them in a roasting tin (pan).

3 Roast the aubergines for about 1 hour until cooked and soft, then remove them from the oven.

4 Place the Feta in a piece of foil, drizzle over half the oil, add the sprig of thyme and season with salt and pepper. Seal in the foil, then place in the hot oven for about 15 minutes while you prepare the aubergines.

5 Peel the aubergines, then roughly chop the flesh with two spoons. Crumble the baked Feta, then stir it into the aubergine with the remaining oil and mix well. Stir in the parsley and season to taste with salt and pepper.

Serving suggestions This is delicious with my Focaccia (see page 138) or any crusty breads.

Hints and variations You can omit the Feta cheese and add 15 ml/ 1 tbsp of tahini paste, which gives the dip an interesting, nutty flavour.

Mediterranean flavour There is a small Greek island called Yali, which means 'glass'. We often had barbecues on its fabulous golden sandy beach where you can find natural glass.

Guacamole dip

A selection of dips and breads looks great on a platter for a drinks party. When I first started work on yachts, you could rarely buy avocados in Greece and those available in Turkey were local ones – tasty but tiny. Now you can buy them everywhere.

SERVES 6–8

2 ripe avocados

Juice of 1 lemon

2 large tomatoes, seeded and diced

1 red (bell) pepper, diced

½ red onion, diced

30 ml/2 tbsp chopped fresh coriander (cilantro)

Salt

A few drops of Tabasco sauce

1 Peel and stone (pit) the avocados and place the flesh in a large mixing bowl. Mash well with a little of the lemon juice to prevent the flesh from turning brown.

2 Mix in the tomatoes, pepper, onion and coriander, then season to taste with salt and the remaining lemon juice. Gradually add the Tabasco, but do it slowly and taste as you go as you do not want the chilli to overpower the dip.

Serving suggestions You can serve this dip in the usual way with a variety of corn chips or toasted tortilla chips. Alternatively, try placing a teaspoonful of the guacamole on individual tortilla chips, then top it with a prawn and some chopped coriander – delicious!

Gazpacho with garlic croûtons

Cooking for a Spanish family on board their motor yacht one year meant I had to make sure my gazpacho was up to their standard. I can now share with you the authentic Spanish tips I learnt from the grandmother of the family.

SERVES 6–8

1.5 kg/3 lb tomatoes

2 sweet white onions

1 cucumber

½ yellow (bell) pepper

½ green pepper

1 garlic clove

150 ml/¼ pint/⅔ cup olive oil

50 ml/2 floz/3 tbsp white wine vinegar

Salt and freshly ground black pepper

About 15 ml/1 tbsp Tabasco sauce

2 hard-boiled (hard-cooked) eggs, finely chopped

FOR THE CROÛTONS

4 slices of bread

1 garlic clove, crushed

45 ml/3 tbsp olive oil

1 Dice two of the tomatoes and one of the onions. Cut the cucumber in half. Set one half aside and cut the other half into julienne strips 3 cm/1¼ in long. Cut the yellow pepper into the same-sized julienne strips.

2 Place the remaining tomatoes in a large bowl, pour over boiling water and leave to stand for about 2 minutes. Carefully lift out the tomatoes and plunge into cold water to loosen the skins so that you can remove them. Core and seed the tomatoes.

3 Blend the tomato flesh in a food processor or blender with the remaining onion and reserved cucumber, the green pepper and the garlic clove, in batches if necessary, until smooth. This can take a few minutes so do not rush to finish it.

4 Add the olive oil and white wine vinegar and blend again.

5 Pour into a bowl, then season to taste with salt and pepper and Tabasco sauce.

6 Chill for at least 2 hours.

7 To make the croûtons, remove the crusts and cut the bread into squares. Heat the garlic in the oil in a frying pan (skillet), then add the bread cubes and fry (sauté) lightly until golden. Remove and drain on kitchen paper (paper towels).

8 Arrange the julienned vegetables and chopped eggs on a serving platter. Spoon the soup into bowls and sprinkle with the croûtons before serving.

Serving suggestions If you don't want to prepare the julienne vegetables, simply serve the gazpacho just as it is. You can also drop a few ice cubes into the soup.

Corn and crab soup with coriander

This is an easy Asian-style soup and, since it can be frozen, it's ideal for dinner parties as you can do all the preparation in advance. The coriander adds colour as well as flavour and looks beautiful if you serve the soup in small oriental-style bowls.

SERVES 6–8

2 corn cobs

1 large red chilli

15 ml/1 tbsp grated fresh root ginger

300 g/11 oz fresh or frozen crabmeat

1 litre/1¾ pts/4¼ cups chicken or vegetable stock

15 ml/1 tbsp cornflour (cornstarch)

100 g/4 oz rice noodles

Salt and freshly ground black pepper

6 spring onions (scallions), chopped

45 ml/3 tbsp chopped fresh coriander (cilantro)

1 Slide the blade of a sharp knife down the corn cobs, cutting off all the kernels.

2 Place half the corn kernels in a blender together with the chilli and ginger and blend.

3 Place the remaining corn in a large saucepan with the crabmeat. Pour over half the stock and bring to a simmer. Add the blended corn mixture and bring to the boil, then simmer for 10 minutes.

4 Blend the cornflour with a little water, then whisk it into the soup and stir until it thickens slightly. Break the noodles into smallish pieces, stir into the soup and simmer for a further 5 minutes until soft.

5 Add enough of the remaining stock to make the soup your preferred consistency and bring to a simmer. Season to taste with salt and pepper and add the spring onions and coriander.

Hints and variations For speed, you can use a 300 g/11 oz/medium can of sweetcorn (corn), drained, instead of the fresh corn cobs. You can also make the soup with cooked chicken instead of the crabmeat.

Prawn omelette rolls

I like to serve these rolls with drinks when we have guests on board – they make a change from sushi and other nibbles. You need to make them in advance so they have time to chill.

SERVES 6–8

4 eggs

120 ml/4 fl oz/½ cup milk

Salt and freshly ground black pepper

30 ml/2 tbsp butter or margarine

100 g/4 oz/½ cup full-fat soft cream cheese

30 ml/2 tbsp tomato ketchup (catsup)

30 ml/2 tbsp Worcestershire sauce

15 ml/1 tbsp Tabasco sauce

100 g/4 oz cooked, peeled prawns (shrimp), chopped

½ red (bell) pepper, cut into julienne strips

½ avocado, cut into julienne strips

4 spring onions (scallions), cut into julienne strips

A few sprigs of fresh parsley, to garnish

1 Beat together the eggs and milk and season well with salt and pepper.

2 Heat a knob of the butter or margarine in a small omelette pan, then pour in just enough of the egg mixture to coat the base of the pan thinly, tilting the pan as you do so to spread the batter. You want each omelette to be as thin as a crêpe. The mixture will bubble up slightly. Allow it to cook for a couple of minutes until set on the underside, then turn over the omelette and cook the other side for a minute or so until lightly golden. Remove from the pan and set aside while you make another five omelettes in the same way.

3 Mix the cream cheese with the tomato ketchup and Worcestershire sauce, then add the Tabasco sauce to taste; use a little less if you don't want it too spicy. Stir in the prawns.

4 Lay the omelettes on a work surface and spread with the prawn mixture, then top with the julienne strips of pepper, avocado and spring onion. Roll them up, cover with clingfilm (plastic wrap) and chill for 30 minutes.

5 Using diagonal, sushi-style cuts, slice the omelette rolls into 2 cm/¾ in pieces and arrange on a serving platter, garnished with sprigs of parsley.

Serving suggestions If you are serving the rolls as a canapé, they are best sliced into small pieces. You can also serve them as a starter, sliced in half at an angle and placed on a green salad.

Marinated calamari salad

*We eat a lot of calamari in the Mediterranean because it is delicious and really easy
to cook. The secret of success is to cook it quickly until it is just tender; if you cook it
for too long, it will go rubbery.*

SERVES 6–8

**4 mangos, peeled, stoned (pitted)
and diced**

Juice of 6 limes

Juice of 2 lemons

1 red onion, chopped

2 chillies, seeded and chopped

**2.5 cm/1 in piece of fresh root ginger,
peeled and grated**

**75 g/3 oz/1½ cups roughly chopped
fresh coriander (cilantro)**

**700 g/1½ lb fresh calamari,
sliced into rings**

**50 g/2 oz/1 cup chopped spring onions
(scallions)**

Salt and freshly ground black pepper

1 Blend two of the mangos to a pulp with half the lime juice, half the
lemon juice, the red onion, chillies and ginger and a third of the
coriander. Transfer to a non-metallic bowl.

2 Bring a large pan of salted water to the boil. Add the calamari rings
for 3 minutes, then drain quickly and add to the mango marinade,
cover and allow to marinate for a few hours.

3 Remove the calamari from the marinade, mix with the remaining
mangos and coriander and the spring onions and arrange on a
serving platter.

4 Strain the marinade, then stir the remaining lime and lemon juices
and pour over the calamari. Season to taste with salt and pepper.

Serving suggestions Serve the calamari mixture just as it is, on a bed
of tossed salad leaves.

Hints and variations You can substitute firm white fish fillets for the
calamari. Do not cook the fish but allow it to cook in the marinade
for 1 hour, then serve it as ceviche with some toasted bread and
crisp salad strips.

Californian sushi

This is a long recipe, but well worth the effort. I always make it when we catch fish at sea, as it is so beautifully fresh. I have given two different fillings here, but there are plenty of other possibilities. I always include vegetarian ones and sometimes some with omelettes.

SERVES 6–8

700 g/1½ lb/3 cups sushi rice

750 ml/1¼ pts/3 cups water

75 ml/5 tbsp rice wine vinegar

5 ml/1 tsp salt

10 ml/2 tsp caster (superfine) sugar

16 raw prawns (shrimp),
shelled and deveined

1 packet of nori seaweed
sheets (10 in all)

2 carrots, cut into julienne strips

3 spring onions (scallions),
cut into julienne strips

1 avocado, thinly sliced

300 g/11 oz fresh tuna fillet,
sliced into 1 cm/½ in strips

60 ml/4 tbsp wasabi paste

1 small punnet of cress

30 ml/2 tbsp sesame seeds

TO SERVE
A little chopped pickled ginger

150 ml/¼ pint/⅔ cup soy sauce

1 Wash the rice three times to remove the excess starch. Place it in a heavy-based saucepan with a lid and add the water. Bring to the boil quickly, then cover and turn the heat down to a gentle simmer. Simmer for 15 minutes, then turn off the heat and allow it to steam for 5 minutes before taking off the lid and covering with a clean tea towel (dish cloth). Leave it for a further 10 minutes to finish.

2 Mix together the rice wine vinegar, salt and sugar in a small pan and dissolve over a low heat, then allow to cool as rice is steaming.

3 Once the rice is cooled, spread it out in a non-metal dish and stir in the vinegar mixture a little at a time until it will not absorb any more; you may not need all the vinegar. Cover the rice with a tea towel once more and leave it to stand at room temperature as you prepare the rest of the ingredients. Do not put in the fridge.

4 Thread the prawns lengthways on to skewers. Bring a large pan of water to the boil, add the prawns and boil for 2 minutes until they turn pink. Remove them from the water and leave to cool. Remove from the skewers, slice in half lengthways and set aside.

5 Lay a tea towel over your work surface and place the sushi mat on top. Have all your ingredients ready, together with a bowl of water. You will need to use wet hands to spread the rice around otherwise it will stick to your fingers and you'll end up in all sorts of trouble!

6 Lay a piece of nori seaweed on the mat. With wet hands, take a handful of rice and spread it over about two-thirds of the nori, leaving an edge uncovered all round. Make a long indentation in the rice about 2 cm/¾ in from the bottom edge and lay four overlapping prawn halves along the gap. Place some pieces of carrot, spring onion and avocado on top.

7 Brush the edges of the nori with a little water, then, using the mat as a guide, roll up the sushi tightly away from you. The wet edges will stick together and seal the sushi roll. Repeat the process until you have used all the prawn filling.

8 Use the same technique to make sushi with the slices of tuna. Spread a little of the wasabi paste in the gap in the rice, then sprinkle it with cress and sesame seeds.

9 Cut the sushi diagonally into 2 cm/¾ in lengths and arrange on a serving platter with little bowls of the remaining wasabi paste, the pickled ginger and the soy sauce for dipping.

Serving suggestions I often serve sushi with some sesame spinach, crispy rice noodles and ceviche, or sashimi. Sushi is best eaten as soon as it is made, but if you are not going to use it immediately, cover loosely with a damp tea towel and clingfilm (plastic wrap).

Hints and variations You should be able to find sushi rice in major supermarkets, but if not, you can use arborio or other medium-grain risotto rice, although it is best if you soak it in cold water for an hour before cooking to remove some of the starch. Wasabi paste is convenient, although I often use wasabi powder as you can make it thicker and mould it into shapes, or dilute it with soy sauce to make a tastier option. I also like to use fish in tempura batter as a filling.

Falafels

These are so easy to make and taste delicious. You can buy ready-mixed falafel flour, but remember that this already contains herbs and spices – and possibly a few other additives as well!

SERVES 6–8

300 g/11 oz/scant 2 cups dried chick peas (garbanzos), soaked overnight in cold water

15 ml/1 tbsp ground cumin

15 ml/1 tbsp ground coriander (cilantro)

50 g/2 oz/1 cup chopped fresh coriander

50 g/2 oz/1 cup chopped fresh parsley

1 onion, finely chopped

1 chilli, seeded and chopped

Salt and freshly ground black pepper

Groundnut (peanut) or corn oil, for cooking

1 Take a handful of the chick peas at a time and lay them in a folded tea towel (dish cloth) and rub them to remove the skins. Make sure you get all the skins off. You can use a rolling pin to break them down a bit before rubbing if it helps.

2 Put the chick peas in a food processor and grind them until fairly fine. Add all the remaining ingredients except the oil and pulse-blend to mix them all together.

3 Leave the mixture to rest for 30 minutes in the fridge.

4 Shape the mixture into walnut-sized balls.

5 Heat a little oil in a frying pan (skillet) and fry (sauté) the falafel for about 10 minutes, turning regularly until they are golden all over. Drain well.

Serving suggestions Serve the falafel with Greek yoghurt or Hummus (see page 10) and a small salad with toasted pitta bread.

Hints and variations I find that drying the chick peas out for 15–20 minutes in the oven at 160°C/325°F/gas 3/fan oven 145°C helps the blending process. Take care, though, because you don't want to cook them rock solid.

Mediterranean flavour This dish can be found all over the Middle East. When sailing through the Suez Canal I found small stalls frying falafel all the time, placing them in pittas and serving them with a mixed salad.

Crostini with roasted tomato and feta

Crostini is a wonderful dish to serve in the summer as it is so quick and easy to prepare and looks brilliant with fresh toppings overflowing on to the plates, tempting everyone to tuck in immediately.

SERVES 6–8

6–8 large Roma tomatoes, cut in half lengthways

Salt and freshly ground black pepper

4 garlic cloves

5 ml/1 tsp dried oregano

5 ml/1 tsp dried thyme

120 ml/4 fl oz/½ cup olive oil

1 day-old loaf of sourdough or country-style bread

135 g/4½ oz/½ cup basil pesto

100 g/4 oz/½ cup Feta cheese, crumbled

10 large basil leaves, torn into pieces

1 Preheat the oven to 200°C/400°F/gas 6/fan oven 180°C.

2 Arrange the tomato halves on a baking (cookie) sheet and sprinkle with salt and pepper. Crush two of the garlic cloves and spread them evenly over the tomato halves, then sprinkle with the dried herbs and drizzle with a little of the olive oil. Cook in the oven for 1 hour, checking them every 20 minutes and reducing the oven temperature once they are starting to brown.

3 Preheat the grill (broiler) on the highest setting while you cut the bread into thick slices, allowing two slices per guest, and brush each side with some of the remaining olive oil. Grill (broil) until browned on both sides.

4 Cut the remaining garlic cloves in half, then rub each side of the toasted bread with them. Spread thinly with the pesto.

5 Remove the tomatoes from the oven and spoon one on to each slice of the prepared toast. Scatter the Feta on top, drizzle with a little more olive oil, then return them to the oven for 5 minutes until they are warmed through and the Feta is beginning to melt slightly.

6 Arrange on a serving platter and sprinkle with the basil leaves.

Serving suggestions You can serve crostini on their own or with a fresh side salad for a more substantial dish.

Spanakopitas

This makes a great snack or hors d'oeuvres, suitable for any occasion. Fresh spinach is available throughout the year in the Med. Beetroot leaves are sometimes cooked in the same way. They are delicious steamed and served with olive oil and lemon juice.

SERVES 6–8

1½ kg/3 lb fresh spinach

4 spring onions (scallions), thinly sliced

50 g/2 oz/1 cup chopped fresh parsley

25 g/1 oz/½ cup chopped fresh dill (dill weed)

25 g/1 oz/½ cup chopped fresh mint

200 g/7 oz/generous ¾ cup Feta cheese, crumbled

Salt and freshly ground black pepper

1 egg, beaten

10 sheets of filo pastry (paste)

120 ml/4 fl oz/½ cup melted butter or olive oil

1 Wash the spinach and remove the stalks. Drain well and dry, then chop finely and place in a large bowl. Add the spring onion and chopped herbs, then the Feta cheese. Mix well and season with a little salt and pepper. Add the egg and mix in well.

2 Cut the filo pastry into strips about 8 x 23 cm/3 x 9 in. As filo pastry is so fine and dries out very quickly make sure you cover the pastry you are not using with clingfilm (plastic wrap) and then a damp tea towel (dish cloth). Take one strip, lay it on the work surface and brush the edges with the melted butter or olive oil.

3 Take a teaspoonful of the spinach mix and place it in the corner closest to you, then take the right-hand corner and take it over to the left edge, making a triangle. Press down on the edge to seal it, then take the left-hand corner and take it over to the right edge and continue folding your triangle up the strip until you get to the end. Seal the end edge well with butter or olive oil, then place on a baking (cookie) sheet that will fit in the fridge. Repeat with the rest of the spinach mix and sheets of pastry.

4 Place the spanakopitas in the fridge for at least 30 minutes.

5 Preheat the oven to 180°C/350°F/gas 4/fan oven 160°C.

6 Bake the spanakopitas in the oven for 20–30 minutes until golden brown.

Serving suggestions The Greeks often serve this as part of a main dish, but I prefer to make these smaller triangles and serve them on a large platter with drinks, either on their own or with a yoghurt and mint dip.

Hints and variations You could use a filling of different cheeses and mint, which is just as delicious!

Fried prosciutto and blueberry salad

Prosciutto is a dried cured Italian ham. There are several types, San Daniel and Prosciutto di Parma being the best ones available. Prosciutto is usually sliced paper-thin and served as an antipasta. See photograph opposite page 24.

SERVES 6–8

120 ml/4 fl oz/½ cup olive oil

300 g/11 oz prosciutto slices

300 g/11 oz mixed salad leaves

100 g/4 oz/1 cup pine nuts, toasted

300 g/11 oz blueberries

60 ml/4 tbsp balsamic vinegar

Salt and freshly ground black pepper

50 g/2 oz/½ cup freshly shaved Parmesan cheese

1 Heat 15 ml/1 tbsp of the olive oil in a frying pan (skillet) and fry (sauté) the prosciutto for a few minutes until it is crisp and golden, being careful not to let it burn. Lift out of the pan with a slotted spoon, reserving the oil, and drain on kitchen paper (paper towels). Crumble the prosciutto into pieces.

2 Toss the salad leaves with the pine nuts and half the blueberries.

3 Put the remaining olive oil and the balsamic vinegar in the pan with the remaining blueberries and seasoning to taste and bring to the boil. Remove from the heat and leave to cool slightly.

4 Sprinkle the crumbled prosciutto over the salad. Pour the blueberry mixture over the top and garnish with the Parmesan shavings. Serve immediately.

Serving suggestions You can serve this delicious salad on its own or with chunks of ciabatta.

Hints and variations A variety of fruits go well with prosciutto; figs and cantaloupe melon are particularly good.

Stuffed courgette flowers with mozzarella

Courgette flowers are not very widely available but if you can find them in a specialist food store – or grow your own – this recipe is well worth trying and I'm sure you'll enjoy them as much as we do!

SERVES 6–8

12 anchovies

150 ml/¼ pint/⅔ cup milk

3 bunches of courgette flowers (at least 24 flowers)

12 sun-dried tomatoes, halved

225 g/8 oz Mozzarella cheese, cut into 24 chunks

350 ml/12 fl oz/1⅓ cups soda water or sparkling mineral water

300 ml/½ pt/1¼ cups lager

100 g/4 oz/1 cup plain (all-purpose) flour

15 ml/1 tbsp cornflour (cornstarch)

Olive oil for shallow-frying

A few basil leaves, to garnish

1 Soak the anchovies in the milk for 20 minutes, then drain and rinse thoroughly to remove all the salt. Cut them in half.

2 Wash the courgette flowers gently, being careful not to break them as they are very fragile.

3 Lay a piece of sun-dried tomato on a piece of Mozzarella, place an anchovy half on top, then gently slide into a courgette flower. Repeat with all the other courgette flowers.

4 Mix the soda or mineral water and lager, then whisk in the flour and cornflour to make a smooth batter, making sure that there are no lumps.

5 Heat a little oil in a frying pan (skillet).

6 Dip the courgette flowers into the batter, being careful not to lose the fillings, then fry (sauté) gently for about 4 minutes until golden, turning once. Remove from the pan with a slotted spoon and drain on kitchen paper (paper towels).

7 Arrange three or four overlapping on individual plates and garnish with basil leaves. Serve immediately.

Serving suggestions You can serve these delicious canapés on their own or on a bed of lettuce.

Hints and variations You can adapt the stuffing to suit your taste by using different cheeses, or using tapenade paste or even salted cod, which makes an interesting alternative although it does takes a little more time to prepare.

Photograph opposite:
Fried Prosciutto and Blueberry Salad
(see page 23)

Courgette fritters with yoghurt

Courgettes are grown all over the Med and are one of the staple vegetables throughout the year, as they are pickled and preserved to be eaten during the winter. There are various types, but you can cook them all in the same way.

SERVES 6–8

4 large courgettes (zucchini)

Salt and freshly ground black pepper

1 large onion, grated

1 large carrot, grated

50 g/2 oz/1 cup chopped fresh mint

50 g/2 oz/1 cup chopped fresh parsley

2 eggs, beaten

25 g/1 oz/¹⁄₄ cup plain (all-purpose) flour

10 ml/2 tsp baking powder

45 ml/3 tbsp olive oil

450 ml/³⁄₄ pt/2 cups Greek yoghurt

A pinch of paprika

1 Grate the courgettes into a colander, sprinkle with salt, then leave to drain for 30 minutes.

2 Squeeze out as much moisture as you can with your hands, then place the courgettes in a large bowl. Add the onion, carrot, mint and parsley and mix well.

3 Beat in the eggs, flour and baking powder. You may need a little more flour if the mixture is very wet. Season well with pepper. Cover and chill for 30 minutes.

4 Heat the oil in a frying pan (skillet). Using two spoons, place small amounts of the mixture into the oil, flatten them with the back of one of the spoons and allow them to cook for a few minutes until golden on one side, then turn them over and cook the other side until golden.

5 Drain well on kitchen paper (paper towels), then serve with Greek yoghurt and a dusting of paprika.

Serving suggestions These fritters can be offered as a starter, or as a delicious snack with drinks.

Hints and variations You can make these simply with the courgettes and herbs, omitting the carrot, if you prefer. Alternatively, you can add 100 g/4 oz/1 cup of crumbled Feta cheese.

Photograph opposite:
Fresh Mussels in a Wine and Cream Sauce
(see page 31)

Tomato tartlets

A quick and easy starter, this works at its delicious best in the middle of summer when the tomatoes and basil are full of flavour. It is beautifully colourful in traditional Italian style.

SERVES 6

250 g/9 oz/1 packet of puff pastry (paste)

450 g/1 lb cherry tomatoes, sliced

10 basil leaves, roughly chopped

Salt and freshly ground black pepper

60 ml/4 tbsp olive oil

225 g/8 oz Mozzarella cheese, sliced

1 Roll out the puff pastry and cut into six rounds, using a saucer as a template. Lay these on greased baking (cookie) sheets, prick all over the centres with a fork, then chill for 30 minutes.

2 Preheat the oven to 180°C/350°F/gas 4/fan oven 160°C.

3 Lay the tomato slices on the pastry, then sprinkle with half the basil leaves. Season with salt and pepper and drizzle with half the olive oil. Bake in the oven for 20 minutes.

4 Remove the tarts from the oven, cover with the Mozzarella slices and sprinkle with the remaining basil leaves. Return to the oven for a further 5 minutes.

5 Remove from the oven, drizzle with the remaining olive oil and season with pepper.

Serving suggestions I like to serve these tarts on a bed of shredded lettuce or some mixed green salad leaves.

Hints and variations You can make the tarts whatever size you want; tiny ones make great party nibbles. If you do not have any fresh basil leaves, pesto is a good alternative and works well. The temperatures I work in are not good for making puff pastry, so I always use frozen. The quality is excellent and it's a lot less time-consuming!

Use different-coloured cherry tomatoes to add colour to a platter if you are serving them as canapés at a drinks party.

Smoked swordfish with tomato dressing

Whenever I am in Sicily I go to the markets there and buy freshly smoked swordfish, as well as the fresh swordfish that is caught all around the island. It has a wonderful firm flesh and fantastic flavour that responds well to this simple presentation.

SERVES 6–8

8 tomatoes, skinned, seeded and finely diced

1 red onion, very finely chopped

25 g/1 oz/¹⁄₂ cup chopped fresh parsley

Juice of 1 lemon

120 ml/4 fl oz/¹⁄₂ cup olive oil

Freshly ground black pepper

400 g/14 oz smoked swordfish, sliced

1 lemon, very thinly sliced

1 Mix together the tomato, onion, parsley, lemon juice and olive oil and season to taste with pepper.

2 Arrange the fish on plates, spoon over some of the tomato dressing and garnish with lemon slices.

Serving suggestions Serve the fish on a bed of salad leaves with fresh bread. To make a complete light lunch, serve with bruschetta.

Hints and variations I do smoke fish and chicken myself but I have yet to master the swordfish flavour! I use tea, rice, lemon and orange zest when I smoke foods, which leaves an interesting flavour in the fish or chicken which can then be served with this tomato dressing.

Mediterranean flavour Smoked swordfish is a speciality of Sicily, where the swordfish are fished in the traditional way by spearing them. The fishermen work in small boats, which always seem too small to me to catch such strong fish. Some men sit high on a scaffolding-style mast, while others lie on a long ladder projecting over the water from the bow ready to spear the fish. This is a sight you will never see outside the Messina Straits, between the 'toe' and the 'football' of Italy.

Prawn risotto balls with lemon and herb mayonnaise

These tasty, unusual little balls make a delicious light meal accompanied by a fresh green salad and a few lemon or lime wedges to squeeze over. You can make them well in advance and leave in the fridge until you are ready to cook them.

SERVES 6–8

Olive oil for shallow-frying

1 onion, finely chopped

4 garlic cloves, crushed

700 g/1½ lb/3 cups risotto (arborio) rice

450 ml/¾ pint/2 cups dry white wine

450 ml/¾ pint/2 cups vegetable stock

750 ml/1¼ pts/3 cups water

250 g/9 oz small cooked, peeled and chopped prawns (shrimp)

25 g/1 oz/½ cup snipped fresh chives

Grated zest of 1 lemon

50 g/2 oz/½ cup freshly grated Parmesan cheese

Salt and freshly ground black pepper

Plain (all-purpose) flour for dusting

1 egg, beaten

100 g/4 oz/2 cups fresh breadcrumbs

1 quantity of Lemon and Herb Mayonnaise (see opposite)

1 Heat 30 ml/2 tbsp of the olive oil in a saucepan and fry (sauté) the onion and garlic for a few minutes until translucent.

2 Add the rice and stir well to coat the grains in the flavoured oil.

3 Mix together the wine, stock and water. Gradually begin to add the liquid to the rice, a ladleful at a time, stirring regularly and waiting until the stock has been absorbed before adding more. This will take about 15–20 minutes.

4 Stir in the prawns, chives, lemon zest and Parmesan and season well with salt and pepper.

5 Spoon the risotto on to a flat dish and leave until cold, then chill it in the fridge for 30 minutes.

6 With wet hands, shape the risotto into golfball-sized balls, roll them in flour, then in beaten egg and then in breadcrumbs. Chill for 30 minutes.

7 Heat a few tablespoonfuls of olive oil in a heavy-based frying pan (skillet) and fry the risotto balls for about 10 minutes until golden on all sides. Drain on kitchen paper (paper towels).

8 As a starter, arrange three or four with a salad on individual plates, together with a spoonful of Lemon and Herb Mayonnaise. As a canapé, arrange them on a bed of lettuce on a large platter, with a pot of the mayonnaise on the side.

Hints and variations You can vary the proportions of water, wine and stock to suit your own taste. It is important to keep your hands wet while you are shaping the rice balls as it makes them much easier to handle.

Home-made mayonnaise

It takes a little time and patience to make mayonnaise, but once you have mastered the art you will wonder why you ever bought ready made. The trick is to keep whisking and add the oil slowly.

MAKES ABOUT 300 ML/½ PT/1¼ CUPS

2 egg yolks

5 ml/1 tsp mustard powder

150 ml/¼ pint/⅔ cups olive oil

150 ml/¼ pint/⅔ cups corn oil

15 ml/1 tbsp lemon juice

Salt

1 Place the egg yolks in a large metal or glass bowl and whisk well with a clean whisk. Whisk in the mustard.

2 Place the oils in a pouring jug or bottle. Very slowly – drop by drop – drizzle the oil into the egg yolks, whisking all the time, until all the oil has been absorbed. It is important to do this very slowly.

3 Once all the oil has been blended in and the consistency is fairly thick, add the lemon juice and season to taste with salt.

4 Cover with clingfilm (plastic wrap) and keep in the fridge until you need it. It will last for a few days.

Hints and variations If you have a blender, you can save yourself a lot of wrist-ache, but do be careful not to overbeat the mixture.

For a delicious Lemon and Herb Mayonnaise, you can fold in about 30 ml/2 tbsp of very finely chopped fresh parsley or dill (dill weed). You can also use the mayo as a base for my delicious Tartare Sauce (see page 44).

Mediterranean flavour I always make fresh mayonnaise while we are sailing. The local olive oil that we can buy in the markets has such a wonderful flavour. When you buy olive oil in the supermarket, it is well worth going for the best quality you can find.

seafood main courses

Our guests like to be served plenty of seafood while they are on board. If we can catch it ourselves, so much the better, but we buy quite a lot from local fishermen who come up to the yachts, and from the local fish markets. These are fun to visit and are full of all sorts of different fish from the smallest varieties to large tuna or swordfish, ready to slice into huge steaks that would feed two to three people. There are also lots of mussel farms and fish farms in the Mediterranean now, partly to compensate for over-fishing over the last few centuries.

Fresh mussels in a wine and cream sauce

In the south of France, most of the restaurants serve moules et frîtes, *mussels and chips. This always seemed like an odd combination to me until I tried it and realised how good the chips are at soaking up the delicious juices. See photograph opposite page 25.*

SERVES 6–8

3 kg/7 lb mussels in their shells

15 ml/1 tbsp olive oil

1 large onion, finely chopped

4 garlic cloves, finely chopped

6 tomatoes, diced

50 g/2 oz/1 cup chopped fresh parsley

Salt and freshly ground black pepper

200 ml/7 fl oz/scant 1 cup white wine

200 ml/7 fl oz/scant 1 cup water

100 ml/4 fl oz/½ cup single (light) cream

1 Soak the mussels in cold water for 2 hours, changing the water at least once, to allow them to expel the sand. Drain and rinse well. Discard any with broken shells and those that do not close when you push the shells together. Scrub off the barnacles, pull out the beards and rinse thoroughly.

2 Heat the olive oil in a large saucepan and fry (sauté) the onion and garlic for a few minutes until the onion is soft and opaque.

3 Add the tomatoes and half the parsley and season with salt and pepper. Pour in the wine and water and bring to the boil.

4 Add the mussels, return the liquid to the boil, then reduce to a simmer. Cover the saucepan and allow to steam for about 5 minutes, shaking the pan occasionally, until all the mussels have opened. Discard any that remain closed.

5 Add the cream and heat through quickly, stirring to mix well.

6 Transfer to a warmed serving dish. Spoon over the juices and vegetables and scatter the remaining parsley over the top.

Serving suggestions I like to serve the mussels with crusty bread and give everyone a spoon to soak up the juices, but you can also accompany them with chips (fries) if you like.

Lobster linguine with fresh tomato sauce

We are very lucky working on yachts as our seafood can be the freshest you will ever eat. Mike, my partner, used to be a crayfisherman in Western Australia, where he taught me how to catch lobsters with pots just 10 minutes off shore.

SERVES 6

FOR THE STOCK
60 ml/4 tbsp olive oil

2 onions, chopped

4 garlic cloves, roughly chopped

6 lobster shells

450 g/1 lb cherry tomatoes

½ bunch of fresh parsley

10 black peppercorns

250 ml/8 fl oz/1 cup white wine

500 ml/17 fl oz/2¼ cups water

FOR THE FRESH TOMATO SAUCE
30 ml/2 tbsp olive oil

2 garlic cloves, lightly crushed

450 g/1 lb cherry tomatoes

Salt and freshly ground black pepper

TO FINISH
1.5 kg/3 lb linguine

1 egg, beaten

250 ml/8 fl oz/1 cup crème fraîche or double (heavy) cream

2 cooked lobsters tails

½ bunch of fresh parsley, finely chopped

1 To make the stock, heat the oil in a large saucepan and fry (sauté) the onions and garlic for a few minutes until soft. Add the lobster shells and tomatoes, stirring well to coat them in oil. Add the parsley and peppercorns.

2 Add the wine and water and bring to the boil. Turn down the heat and simmer for 40 minutes, stirring regularly.

3 Turn off the heat and allow to cool and infuse all the flavours.

4 Strain the stock and discard everything except the liquid. Return to a clean pan, bring to the boil and boil rapidly until reduced by half.

5 Meanwhile, make the tomato sauce. Heat the oil in a saucepan and fry the garlic for a few minutes until soft. Add the tomatoes and simmer for 30 minutes, stirring occasionally. Season to taste with salt and pepper. Use a wooden spoon to rub the sauce through a sieve (strainer).

6 Bring a large pan of lightly salted water to the boil. Add the pasta, bring to the boil and simmer for about 8 minutes until just cooked.

7 Add the sauce to the reduced stock. Warm the sauce but do not allow it to boil. Season to taste with salt and pepper.

8 Beat the egg with the crème fraîche or cream and stir it into the sauce until it thickens. Do not allow to boil, or it will curdle. Remove the meat from the lobster tails, chop and add to the sauce.

9 Drain the pasta and place in a warmed serving dish. Pour over the sauce, toss together gently, then serve sprinkled with the parsley.

Serving suggestions A fresh mixed salad is all you need to accompany this dish.

Seafood paella

The name 'paella' comes from the dish in which it is traditionally made, so it is usual to serve it straight from the cooking dish. You can surround the dish with smaller dishes containing the garnishes.

SERVES 6–8

45 ml/3 tbsp olive oil

2 onions, thinly sliced

4 garlic cloves, crushed

2 chicken breasts, sliced

1.2 litres/2 pts/5 cups fish stock

8 saffron strands

700 g/1½ lb/3 cups paella or medium-grain rice

4 white fish fillets, such as sea bass

700 g/1½ lb calamari, cut into rings

700 g/1½ lb prawns (shrimp)

700 g/1½ lb mussels in their shells, scrubbed and bearded

250 ml/8 fl oz/1 cup white wine

4 celery stalks, roughly chopped

Salt and freshly ground black pepper

50 g/2 oz/1 cup chopped fresh parsley

FOR THE GARNISH
2 lemons, cut into quarters

4 celery sticks, cut into chunks

8–10 radishes

1 small sweet white onion, sliced

1 Preheat the oven to 180°C/350°F/gas 4/fan oven 160°C.

2 Heat 15 ml/1 tbsp of the olive oil in a paella pan or large ovenproof frying pan (skillet) and fry (sauté) the onions and garlic for a few minutes until soft. Remove from the pan and set aside.

3 Add a further 15 ml/1 tbsp of the oil to the pan and fry the chicken for about 10 minutes until only just cooked. Remove from the pan and set aside.

4 Warm the stock. Put a little in a small bowl, add the saffron strands and allow to infuse for a few minutes while you start to cook the rice.

5 Add the remaining oil to the pan, stir in the rice and continue to stir until the grains are shiny and well coated. Gradually begin to add the stock a ladleful at a time, stirring continuously and allowing the rice to absorb the liquid before adding more.

6 When you have added about half the stock, add the fish fillets, calamari, prawns and mussels. Add the remaining stock, the saffron stock, wine and celery, and season with salt and pepper. Cover the dish with a lid or foil, then place in the oven for 20–30 minutes until the rice is tender.

7 Remove from the oven and take off the foil. Stir well and sprinkle with the parsley.

8 Arrange the lemon wedges, celery pieces, radishes and white onion slices on a large platter or in individual bowls and serve with the paella.

Hints and variations If you have a good fish stock, that is perfect for making paella, but chicken or vegetable stock will work very well too. While you are scrubbing the mussels, tap them sharply and discard any that do not close.

Marinated prawns with onions, peppers and capers

You must start this recipe in advance as it needs at least 12 hours to marinate the prawns. The fresh herbs add a great contrast to the colours here and arranging some sprigs on the rice, if you are serving it, adds a wonderful final touch.

SERVES 6–8

250 ml/8 fl oz/1 cup cider vinegar or white wine vinegar

120 ml/4 fl oz/½ cup lemon juice

60 ml/4 tbsp lime juice

30 ml/2 tbsp Tabasco or chilli sauce

30 ml/2 tbsp wholegrain or Dijon mustard

120 ml/4 fl oz/½ cup olive oil, plus extra for shallow-frying

2 kg/4½ lb raw king prawns (jumbo shrimp)

2 yellow (bell) peppers, thinly sliced

2 red onions, thinly sliced

1 chilli, thinly sliced

30 ml/2 tbsp capers, rinsed and drained (optional)

25 g/1 oz/½ cup chopped fresh parsley

25 g/1 oz/½ cup chopped fresh coriander (cilantro)

1 Place the vinegar, lemon and lime juices, Tabasco sauce, mustard and measured olive oil in a non-metal bowl and whisk together well.

2 Peel the prawns, leaving on the tails, and use a sharp knife to remove the vein down the back. Add to the marinade with the peppers, onions, chilli and capers. Cover with clingfilm (plastic wrap) and leave to marinate for 12–24 hours, stirring occasionally, so that all the prawns are evenly covered in the marinade.

3 Remove the prawns, peppers and onions from the marinade.

4 Heat 30 ml/2 tbsp olive oil in a large heavy-based frying pan (skillet) and quickly fry (sauté) the prawns and vegetables just until the prawns turn pink.

5 Toss with the fresh chopped herbs and serve at once.

Serving suggestions Serve the prawns on a bed of green salad with fresh bread or plain boiled rice.

To make a wonderful table piece, use a dariole mould to form the rice in the centre of a platter and spoon the prawns and vegetables around.

Hints and variations I often substitute lemon or lime juice for the cider vinegar or white wine vinegar.

Seafood curry with coconut cream, ginger, garlic and cumin

I enjoy making curries – so much so that I usually find that I do far too much for one meal! My father was brought up in India and when I was growing up we would eat curries at least once a week. We still continue the tradition because we love the flavours.

SERVES 6–8

2.5 ml/½ tsp black peppercorns

15 ml/1 tbsp coriander (cilantro) seeds

15 ml/1 tbsp olive oil

15 ml/1 tbsp black mustard seeds

1 onion, thinly sliced

3 garlic cloves, crushed

10 ml/2 tsp grated fresh root ginger

1–2 fresh chillies, sliced open

15 ml/1 tbsp paprika

2.5 ml/½ tsp chilli powder

2.5 ml/½ tsp ground turmeric

2 curry leaves (optional)

Juice of ½ lemon

3 tomatoes, roughly chopped

200 ml/7 fl oz/1 small can of coconut milk

Salt and freshly ground black pepper

1 kg/2¼ lb raw prawns (shrimp), shelled and deveined

500 g/18 oz fish fillets, skinned and cut into 1 cm/½ in pieces

25 g/1 oz/½ cup chopped fresh coriander

1 Place the black peppercorns and coriander seeds in a small dry frying pan (skillet) and toss over a medium heat for a few minutes until fragrant, making sure they don't burn. Grind them finely using a pestle and mortar.

2 Heat the oil in a large frying pan and fry (sauté) the mustard seeds until they start to pop, then stir in the onion and garlic and fry for a few minutes until they are browning slightly. Add the peppercorn mixture, the ginger, chillies, paprika, chilli powder, turmeric, curry leaves, if using, and lemon juice and stir to mix well.

3 Stir in the tomatoes and bring to the boil, then add the coconut milk. Bring to a simmer and simmer for a few minutes. Adjust the seasoning to taste.

4 Add the prawns and fish and cook gently for a few minutes before serving with the chopped coriander scattered over. If you are not ready to serve immediately, you can keep the curry warm but do not bring it back to the boil again. If it looks too dry, add a cup of water.

Serving suggestions This looks great in a large, shallow pasta bowl with rice to one side. I like to serve it with boiled rice, lime pickle and mango chutney.

Hints and variations The open chillies will make the curry very spicy – if you prefer a milder version, remove the seeds.

Rice wrappers with prawns and dipping sauce

You can buy rice wrappers in oriental stores to use for spring rolls. Sunflower shoots may be hard to find. I serve these as starters or as a main course – they look and taste great.

SERVES 6

24 raw prawns (shrimp),
shelled and deveined

100 g/4 oz rice noodles

12 rice wrappers

½ yellow (bell) pepper, finely diced

3 carrots, cut into julienne strips

1 small cucumber, skinned and
cut into julienne strips

1 chilli, finely chopped

1 bunch of sunflower shoots (optional)

100 g/4 oz/2 cups fresh coriander
(cilantro) leaves

1 bunch of spring onions (scallions)

FOR THE DIPPING SAUCE
120 ml/4 fl oz/½ cup sweet chilli sauce

250 ml/8 fl oz/1 cup lime juice

10 ml/2 tsp Thai fish sauce

1 Thread the prawns on to 12 skewers. Bring a large pan of water to the boil, add the skewers and cook for a few minutes until the prawns are pink, then remove and run under cold water to stop the cooking. Take them off the skewers, cut in half lengthways and set aside.

2 Place the noodles in a large bowl, pour over some boiling water and leave to cook for a few minutes. Drain and place in iced water until you need them. (You can cut the rice noodles into smaller lengths to make them easier to use.)

3 Soften the rice wrappers by placing them in a bowl of water or brushing with water on both sides.

4 Place a dampened wrapper on the work surface. Add two prawns halves, some diced pepper, carrot, cucumber, chilli, sunflower shoots, if using, coriander, spring onions and a few noodles, then two more prawn halves. Arrange in a fan shape in the centre of the wrap, leaving the bottom third without any filling.

5 Fold the empty third of the wrap up over the base of the fan of vegetables and prawns, enclosing them so that you can roll the wrap up into a conical shape. It doesn't matter if a few of the ingredients hang out of the wrap. Place it on a large plate and cover it with a damp tea towel (dish cloth) while you make the rest.

6 To make the sauce, mix together all the ingredients in a bowl.

7 Arrange the wraps on a serving platter, drizzle a little of the sauce over, then offer the remaining sauce in individual bowls.

Serving suggestions Plain rice and a large, crisp green salad make a perfect meal.

Hints and variations The rice paper wraps can also be used to make spring rolls that are deep-fried, so experiment with uncooked prawn or chicken fillings.

Sweet chilli prawns with a mixed salad

This dish is just bursting with flavours, with the freshness of the orange and the vegetables providing a wonderful contrast to the spices. It makes a delicious and refreshing dish.

SERVES 6–8

500 ml/17 fl oz/2¼ cups orange juice

36 large raw prawns (jumbo shrimp), shelled and deveined

4 carrots, cut into julienne strips

2 red (bell) peppers, cut into julienne strips

1 Chinese cabbage, thinly sliced

100 g/4 oz/1 cup coriander (cilantro) seeds

10 ml/2 tsp mustard seeds

10 ml/2 tsp dried chillies

10 ml/2 tsp red peppercorns

10 ml/2 tsp black peppercorns

FOR THE DRESSING

500 ml/17 fl oz/2¼ cups orange juice

15 ml/1 tbsp balsamic vinegar

15 ml/1 tbsp sweet chilli sauce

30 ml/2 tbsp olive oil

Salt and freshly ground black pepper

TO FINISH

120 ml/4 fl oz/½ cup chilli olive oil

2 garlic cloves, crushed

50 g/2 oz/1 cup chopped fresh coriander

1 Pour the orange juice over the prawns and toss well. Allow to marinate for a few hours or as long as possible.

2 Soak the carrots and pepper in iced water for 30 minutes. Drain well and dry with a tea towel (dish cloth). Transfer to a serving dish and mix in the Chinese cabbage.

3 Heat a small frying pan (skillet) and dry-fry the coriander and mustard seeds, dried chillies and red and black peppercorns until fragrant, then crush them using a pestle and mortar.

4 Drain the prawns well and toss them in the crushed spices.

5 Whisk together the dressing ingredients and toss with the vegetables.

6 Heat the chilli oil and fry (sauté) the prawns and garlic quickly until just cooked. Stir in the fresh coriander.

7 Spoon the prawn mixture over the salad, then serve.

Serving suggestions I like to serve this with a crisp mixed green salad and plenty of popadoms. If you have a deep-fryer, you can shape the popadoms as they cook so that they form small baskets. Place a small amount of rice in each one, add the prawns and set the whole thing on a bed of mixed leaves with the crispy vegetable salad.

Grilled calamari with garlic and parsley

Calamari make a great summer lunch – especially when cooked this way.
They are especially good if you can barbecue them as it imparts that wonderfully
subtle smoky flavour.

SERVES 6–8

150 g/5 oz Emmental (Swiss) cheese

1 bunch of spring onions (scallions)

1 bunch of fresh dill (dill weed), cut into
small sprigs

700 g/1½ lb small calamari, cleaned

Salt and freshly ground black pepper

150 ml/¼ pt/⅔ cup olive oil

45 ml/3 tbsp chopped fresh parsley

1 garlic clove, crushed

1 Slice the cheese and spring onions into pieces that will fit inside the calamari.

2 Place a piece of cheese, onion and dill inside each calamari and season well with salt and pepper.

3 Heat the grill (broiler) or barbecue and cook the calamari for just a few minutes until tender. Don't leave them too long or they can become tough.

4 Meanwhile, whisk together the olive oil, parsley and garlic.

5 Arrange the calamari on warm plates and drizzle over the dressing before serving.

Serving suggestions You can serve the calamari on a bed of rocket or your favourite salad leaves, and perhaps squeeze over some fresh lemon juice. Alternatively, mix lots of chopped parsley with some crushed garlic, grated lemon rind and olive oil and pour over the calamari. Accompany with lots of fresh crusty bread.

Mediterranean flavour Not surprisingly, the fish markets in Mediterranean towns are often near the marina. (On one occasion we went by taxi as we didn't know where it was, only to find out – having parted with the taxi fare – that it was just round the corner!)

The markets are often held in the evenings, like the one at Gaeta in Italy, where you will find the stalls spread out along the waterfront, selling all sorts of wonderful fresh seafood: clams, mussels, prawns (shrimp), scampi, sea bass, red mullet, sardines, eels and all kinds of other fish from the local waters. People just draw up on mopeds or in their cars alongside the market and buy what they want.

Crab cakes with aioli

Try to get Thai mint for this dish – it has a wonderful, unusual flavour. I love to use fresh crabmeat, both the brown and white meat if I can get it, though that's often hard in the Mediterranean. If you can't get fresh crabmeat you can use frozen – but not canned.

SERVES 6–8

700 g/1½ lb fresh crabmeat

1 bunch of spring onions (scallions), chopped

25 g/1 oz/½ cup chopped fresh parsley

25 g/1 oz/½ cup chopped fresh coriander (cilantro)

25 g/1 oz/½ cup chopped fresh mint

4 large potatoes, parboiled and grated

1 small fresh chilli, seeded and chopped

2.5 cm/1 in piece of fresh root ginger, peeled and grated

Salt and freshly ground black pepper

1 egg, beaten

100 g/4 oz/1 cup plain (all-purpose) flour

30 ml/2 tbsp olive oil

2 oz/50 g/¼ cup butter or margarine

FOR THE AIOLI
1 garlic clove

A pinch of salt

375 ml/13 fl oz/1½ cups mayonnaise

15 ml/1 tbsp snipped fresh chives

A squeeze of lemon juice

1 Flake the crabmeat into a bowl and mix in the spring onions, parsley, coriander, mint, potatoes, chilli and ginger. Season well.

2 Add the beaten egg and stir in enough of the flour to give a fairly sticky mixture. You may need more or less than the quantity given. Dust your hands with a little more flour and form the mixture into 16 cakes. Place them on a baking (cookie) sheet, cover with clingfilm (plastic wrap) and chill for at least 30 minutes.

3 Preheat the oven to 200°C/400°F/gas 6/fan oven 180°C.

4 Heat the oil and butter or margarine in a frying pan (skillet) and fry (sauté) the crabcakes for a few minutes until just golden on both sides. Place on a baking sheet and cook in the oven for 10 minutes.

5 To make the aioli, crush the garlic with the salt, then blend well into the mayonnaise. Add the chives and season with a squeeze of lemon juice and some pepper. Tip into a small serving bowl.

6 Arrange the crab cakes on a large serving platter and serve with the aioli.

Serving suggestions As well as serving them as a lunch dish with salad and bread, I like to serve these small crabcakes on their own as canapés or a tasty starter. I arrange them on a bed of rocket with a portion of aioli and some lime or lemon wedges. You can also serve them with mango salsa, or choose a selection of your favourite dipping sauces.

Hints and variations The above method of making aioli is the 'cheat's' method and very easy to do at any time, especially if you have ready-made mayonnaise in your fridge. To make real aioli, you need to blend mashed potato into the mixture as you are making the mayonnaise.

Teriyaki salmon with asparagus and ginger

*This impressive dish is rich in flavours and colours so it needs no accompaniments.
It is best simply complemented with a bowl of steamed rice or rice noodles.*

SERVES 6–8

6–8 salmon fillets

**7.5 cm/3 in piece of fresh root ginger,
peeled and grated**

1 garlic clove, crushed

250 ml/8 fl oz/1 cup teriyaki sauce

3 bunches of asparagus, trimmed

60 ml/4 tbsp olive oil

1 Place the salmon in a large glass dish that will hold them all in a single layer. Mix half the ginger with the garlic and teriyaki sauce. Pour this over the fish, cover and leave to marinate in the fridge for 1 hour.

2 Bring a large pan of water to the boil, add the bunches of asparagus and blanch for 1 minute. Drain and run under cold water to keep the colour.

3 Grill (broil) the asparagus for a few minutes until they are coloured on all sides. Keep them warm while you prepare the rest of the dish.

4 Heat half the olive oil in a non-stick frying pan (skillet). Remove the fish from the marinade and sear on the skin side for about 4 minutes, then turn and cook for 2 minutes on the other side. Transfer to a dish and keep warm.

5 Pour the marinade into the pan and heat through.

6 Heat the remaining oil in a separate pan and fry (sauté) the remaining ginger for a few minutes until crisp and golden.

7 Arrange the asparagus in a fan on each plate, then place a salmon fillet on top. Spoon over some of the sauce, top with the fried ginger and serve immediately.

Serving suggestions The fish looks very impressive simply served on its own, with individual bowls of rice on the side.

Hints and variations When asparagus is hard to find, I use baby leeks or even spring onions as the bed for the salmon to lay on.

If you want to make your own teriyaki sauce, simply mix 150 ml/ ¼ pt/⅔ cup soy sauce with 100 ml/3½ fl oz/scant ½ cup dry sherry or mirin and 45 ml/3 tbsp clear honey.

Thai fish cakes with dipping sauce

The flavours of Thai cooking are perfect for fish, and of course we are never far from a fish market when we're cruising in the Med. This recipe will work for almost any kind of firm white fillets.

SERVES 6–8

FOR THE FISH CAKES

1 bunch of fresh coriander (cilantro), finely chopped

1 bunch of spring onions (scallions), finely chopped

2 chillies, seeded and finely chopped

1 stalk of lemon grass, chopped

4 cm/1½ in piece of fresh root ginger, peeled and grated

Grated zest of 1 lime

900 g/2 lb firm white fish fillets

Salt and freshly ground black pepper

30 ml/2 tbsp olive oil

FOR THE SAUCE

100 g/4 oz/½ cup caster (superfine) sugar

250 ml/8 fl oz/1 cup water

1 chilli, finely chopped

15 ml/1 tbsp Thai fish sauce

50 g/2 oz/1 cup chopped fresh coriander

½ small cucumber, skinned and cut into paper-thin slices

1 To make the fish cakes, mix together the coriander, spring onions, chillies, lemon grass, ginger and lime zest.

2 Place the fish in a blender and pulse quickly so that it is broken up but not mushy. Alternatively, flake very finely with a fork. Add to the herbs and spices, season to taste and mix well.

3 Shape the fish mixture into 16 balls, flattening them slightly, then place on a baking (cookie) sheet, cover and chill for at least 30 minutes to absorb all the flavours. They can be left in the fridge for much longer if you have time.

4 Preheat the oven to 180°C/350°F/gas 4/fan oven 160°C.

5 Heat the oil in a frying pan (skillet) and fry (sauté) the fish cakes for a few minutes until golden on both sides, then return to the baking sheet, cover with foil and cook in the oven for 10 minutes.

6 While they are cooking, place the sugar, water and chilli in a saucepan and bring to the boil. Lower the heat and simmer until the sugar has dissolved. Allow to cool, then add the Thai fish sauce.

7 When ready to serve, arrange the fish cakes on a large serving platter. Stir the coriander and cucumber into the sauce and serve immediately with the fish cakes.

Serving suggestion: I like to accompany the fish with plain rice and an exotic salad of greens and herbs or tropical fruits. I give each guest an individual bowl of dipping sauce.

Hints and variations As a party piece, pierce each fish cake with a lemon grass stalk and use it as a skewer.

Tuna steaks with roasted vegetables and potatoes

The tuna looks really appetising, seared with golden-brown lines over the face of the steaks, so they are perfect for the barbecue or griddle pan. The colours of the roasted vegetables contrast wonderfully with the steaks.

SERVES 6–8

1½ kg/3 lb potatoes

120 ml/4 fl oz/½ cup olive oil, plus extra for brushing

Salt and freshly ground black pepper

3 red (bell) peppers, cut into large pieces

3 yellow peppers, cut into large pieces

6 courgettes (zucchini), diced

2 aubergines (eggplants), diced

3 onions, roughly chopped

450 g/1 lb cherry tomatoes

4 garlic cloves, crushed

6–8 tuna steaks

45 ml/3 tbsp balsamic vinegar

50 g/2 oz/½ cup freshly shaved Parmesan cheese (optional)

1 Preheat the oven to 200°C/400°F/gas 6/fan oven 180°C.

2 Cut the potatoes into 2 cm/¾ in dice and place in a baking dish. Pour over half the olive oil, toss together to coat and season with salt and pepper. Roast in the oven for 30 minutes.

3 Toss the peppers, courgettes, aubergines, onions, tomatoes and garlic with the remaining olive oil in a separate baking dish, season with salt and pepper, and place in the oven with the potatoes for a further 30 minutes until all the vegetables are tender and browned.

4 Meanwhile, heat a grill (broiler) or chargrill pan. Season the tuna steaks with salt and pepper, then brush with a little more olive oil. Grill (broil) for about 4 minutes on each side until tender but still pink on the inside.

5 Mix the balsamic vinegar into the vegetables.

6 Place the tuna steaks on top of the potatoes, then surround them with the roasted vegetables. Sprinkle with shavings of Parmesan, if liked, and serve.

Serving suggestions Simply garnish each plate with a slice of lemon on the side and scatter some chopped parsley around the plate.

Mediterranean flavour When we are sailing in the Mediterranean, we always put out fishing lines. Catching fish is a wonderful experience, which I find very exciting, and of course it is great to cook fish that's as fresh as it is possible to be!

Hash-brown sea bass with passion fruit sauce

We eat a lot of sea bass in the Mediterranean – it is one of the most popular farmed fish and is therefore generally readily available in the markets. It is a tasty white-fleshed fish that is very versatile in cooking as it does not dry out too quickly.

SERVES 8

75 g/3 oz/⅓ cup butter

30 ml/2 tbsp olive oil

3 onions, sliced

50 g/2 oz/½ cup pine nuts

50 g/2 oz/⅓ cup raisins

50–75 g/2–3 oz/¼–⅓ cup soft brown sugar

Salt and freshly ground black pepper

8 passion fruit

2 large potatoes

6 fillets of sea bass, skin left on

1 Melt 25 g/1 oz/2 tbsp of the the butter in a heavy-based saucepan, add half the olive oil and heat. Add the onions and fry (sauté) gently until softened, then add the pine nuts and raisins. Cover and cook gently for 20 minutes, stirring occasionally to ensure that nothing sticks.

2 Add the sugar, stirring until it dissolves. Season to taste with salt and pepper. You can also add a little more sugar if you wish, but do so sparingly – too much will spoil the dish. Keep this mixture warm while you prepare the rest of the dish.

3 Cut each passion fruit in half, then scoop out the flesh and strain the juice and seeds through a metal sieve (strainer). Use a wooden spoon to push as much juice out of the pulp as you can. Do not worry if the juice is sharp as it will soften with the addition of butter and complement the fish like a lemon juice.

4 Warm the passion fruit juice in a small pan, then gradually whisk in the remaining butter a little at a time.

5 Put the potatoes in a pan and bring to the boil. Cook for 8 minutes, then drain and run under cold water until cool enough to handle. Grate on to a plate and season with salt and pepper.

6 Slash the skin of the sea bass slightly (this will prevent the fish from curling up while cooking). Press some of the grated potato on to the flesh-side of each fish fillet.

7 Heat the remaining olive oil in a frying pan (skillet), place the fish potato-side down in the pan and cook gently for about 4 minutes until golden, then turn and cook on the skin-side for 4 minutes.

8 Arrange the sea bass on plates, spoon over some of the caramelised onions and then drizzle over the passion fruit sauce before serving.

Serving suggestions Rice and a green salad go well with this dish, or lightly steamed vegetables.

Spiedino di pesce

I call this dish by its Italian name as it sounds so much more interesting than just 'fish skewers'! We ate plenty of spiedini *in Viareggio at a great beach-front restaurant while we were there with the boat.*

SERVES 6–8

120 ml/4 fl oz/½ cup **lemon juice**

120 ml/4 fl oz/½ cup **olive oil**

50 g/2 oz/1 cup **finely chopped mixed fresh herbs**

Salt and freshly ground black pepper

24 **king prawns (jumbo shrimp)**

450 g/1 lb **swordfish fillet**

300 g/11 oz **calamari**

FOR THE TARTARE SAUCE
2 **egg yolks**

15 ml/1 tbsp **lemon juice**

5 ml/1 tsp **made mustard**

150 ml/¼ pt/⅔ cup **olive oil**

150 ml/¼ pt/⅔ cup **corn oil**

30 ml/2 tbsp **capers, rinsed, drained and chopped**

30 ml/2 tbsp **chopped pickled onions**

15 ml/1 tbsp **cornichons, chopped**

1 Soak eight wooden skewers in water for at least 30 minutes. This will stop them from burning when you place them on the grill (broiler).

2 Whisk together the lemon juice and olive oil. Add the mixed herbs and season with salt and pepper to make the marinade.

3 Peel the prawns, leaving their tails on. Cut the fish and calamari into chunks. Thread the seafood alternately on to the soaked skewers and place in a glass or ceramic dish. Pour over the marinade and leave to marinate for at least 30 minutes.

4 Heat the grill or barbecue and grill (broil) the skewers for about 10 minutes until cooked through and golden.

5 To make the tartare sauce, beat the egg yolks with the lemon juice, mustard and a little of the olive oil, then gradually beat in the remaining olive oil and the corn oil a drop at a time until the mixture thickens. Stir in the capers, onions and cornichons and season to taste.

6 Put the skewers of fish on warm plates and serve the tartare sauce in a small bowl on the side or spooned around the skewers.

Serving suggestions Arrange on a bed of plain rice and accompany with a mixed salad.

Hints and variations Don't be tempted to use all olive oil in the tartare sauce – the flavour is too strong and will overwhelm the taste.

Mediterranean flavour Sailing through the Messina Straits can sometimes be an eventful trip, with different currents and winds meeting there as well as all the ferries and boats coming and going. On clear days it is fun to be able to cruise close to the mainland.

Marinated swordfish salad

Leaving the salad overnight really helps to bring out all the flavours. However, if you don't have time, just leave it as long as you can. It will still be delicious and everyone will enjoy it.

SERVES 6–8

4 large swordfish steaks

120 ml/4 fl oz/½ cup olive oil, plus extra for shallow-frying

45 ml/3 tbsp capers, rinsed, drained and chopped

4 spring onions (scallions), finely chopped

Salt and freshly ground black pepper

120 ml/4 fl oz/½ cup lemon juice

6 large tomatoes, seeded and diced

Wedges of lemon, to garnish

50 g/2 oz/1 cup chopped fresh parsley

1 Heat a large frying pan (skillet) and fry (sauté) the swordfish steaks in a little oil for about 5 minutes on each side until cooked through. Leave to cool, then break up into chunks.

2 Add the capers and spring onions, season with salt and plenty of pepper and mix well.

3 Whisk together the measured olive oil and the lemon juice. Pour over the fish and mix in well. Cover and leave to marinate overnight.

4 At least half an hour before serving, remove the fish from the fridge to allow it to come back to room temperature. Toss a few times and add the diced tomatoes and half the parsley.

5 Serve garnished with lemon wedges and scattered generously with the remaining chopped parsley.

Serving suggestions Arrange on a bed of lettuce leaves on a large serving platter. Plain potatoes or rice make a good accompaniment.

Hints and variations You can also use other fish such as grouper or snapper instead of swordfish, with equally delicious results. This works as a main course or a starter, and could also be adapted as a canapé, with the chunks served wrapped in a lettuce or endive leaf.

Mediterranean flavour The last time I made this was with swordfish bought in Sorrento and it always reminds me of that wonderful trip.

Seared swordfish with sicilian tomato sauce

Another simple but delicious recipe. The best way to cook the swordfish is to make sure the pan is really hot before you add the fish so that the fish is cooked very quickly and does not dry out. Barbecuing will give it an even better flavour.

SERVES 6–8

30 ml/2 tbsp olive oil

2 onions, finely chopped

6 garlic cloves, crushed

1½ kg/3 lb tomatoes, skinned and roughly chopped

30 ml/2 tbsp capers, rinsed and drained

2 oz/50 g/½ cup chopped black olives

Salt and freshly ground black pepper

6–8 swordfish steaks

2 oz/50 g/1 cup chopped fresh mint

1 Heat the oil and fry (sauté) the onions and garlic for a few minutes until just soft. Add the tomatoes, bring to a simmer and cook gently for 30 minutes.

2 Add the capers and olives and season with salt and pepper. Keep warm.

3 Heat the grill (broiler) to its highest setting, then sear the swordfish for a few minutes on each side, making sure you do not overcook it. Alternatively, you can cook it in a grill pan.

4 Stir the mint into the sauce.

5 Pour over the fish and serve.

Serving suggestions Dress the plates with wild rice and set the swordfish on top before spooning over the tomato sauce. You can garnish with some fresh mint leaves for extra colour.

Mediterranean flavour The Sicilians are keen fishermen and have huge nets that span several kilometres, often with lights attached so they can be seen and avoided at night. On one trip, the boat I was sailing on became entangled in an unlit net. We couldn't start the engine in case the net was wound round the propellor and, with the wind behind us, we had to be really careful with the sails as someone cut the net away. Fortunately the net fell away once we had cut it free and we could continue to sail on.

Stuffed sardines

Sardines are sold at fish markets all over the Mediterranean. I particularly like buying them in southern Italy around Naples as you will often find them already scaled, gutted and boned. You can, of course, buy them whole.

SERVES 8

36 fresh sardines

30 ml/2 tbsp olive oil

2 onions, very finely chopped

5 ml/1 tsp minced (ground) garlic

4 oz/100 g/2 cups fresh breadcrumbs

75 g/3 oz/¹/₂ cup raisins, roughly chopped

Juice and grated zest of 4 oranges

2 oz/50 g/¹/₂ cup pine nuts, toasted and chopped

50 g/2 oz/1 cup chopped fresh parsley

Salt and freshly ground black pepper

Wedges of lemon or orange, to garnish

1 Preheat the oven to 180°C/350°F/gas 4/fan oven 160°C.

2 Clean the fish if this has not already been done: remove the heads, then slit open down the belly and remove the guts. Splay the fish out flat, skin-side up, and gently push down on the backbone, which will dislodge it from the flesh. Pull out the backbone, leaving the tail on the fish.

3 Heat the oil in a large frying pan (skillet) and fry (sauté) the onions and garlic gently until they are soft and opaque. Remove from the pan.

4 Add the breadcrumbs to the pan and fry until they are toasted and golden. Allow to cool, then mix in the fried onions and garlic, the raisins, orange zest, half the orange juice, the pine nuts and parsley. Season well with salt and pepper.

5 Place the sardines skin-side down on the work surface, place a spoonful of the filling on each sardine and roll it up. Arrange them tightly in a greased baking tin (pan) and place in the oven for 20 minutes.

6 Pour the rest of the orange juice over the sardines and serve garnished with wedges of lemon or orange.

Serving suggestions Accompany with a fresh green salad.

Hints and variations If the sardines are very small, it may be difficult to roll them up, so instead I spread the stuffing along the fish and place another one on top, then cook them sandwiched in pairs.

Deep-fried salted cod with skordalia

I learned about this dish when I was working out in Greece and really enjoying it. You do need to start a couple of days ahead in order to soak the fish to remove the salt, but it is well worth it. Salted cod is available from delicatessens.

SERVES 6–8

1½ kg/3 lb salted cod fillets

350 g/12 oz/3 cups plain (all-purpose) flour

A pinch of cornflour (cornstarch)

250 ml/8 fl oz/1 cup soda water or sparkling mineral water

375 ml/13 fl oz/1½ cups beer

Salt and freshly ground black pepper

Olive oil for deep-frying

400 g/14 oz potatoes

4 slices of stale bread, crusts removed

6 garlic cloves, crushed

150 ml/¼ pt/⅔ cup olive oil

Wedges of lemon, to garnish

1 Soak the cod in cold water for at least 48 hours, changing the water several times a day to remove the salt.

2 Rinse the fish, then pat dry on kitchen paper (paper towels) or a clean tea towel (dish cloth) to get rid of the excess water. Cut the fish into portions.

3 Whisk together the flour, cornflour, soda or mineral water and beer until smooth. Season with salt and pepper.

4 Heat the oil in a large saucepan or deep-fat fryer. Dip the fish in the batter, then lower it gently into the hot oil and cook for about 8 minutes until it is crisp and golden.

5 To make the skordalia, place the potatoes in a saucepan, cover with water, add a pinch of salt and bring to the boil. Simmer for about 15 minutes until soft enough to be mashed. Drain well and place in a large bowl.

6 Make the bread into breadcrumbs in a food processor or blender.

7 Mash the potatoes until they are very even and soft. This is best done using a hand-blender. Still running the blender, gradually add the garlic and olive oil. When almost all the oil has been incorporated, add the breadcrumbs and season well, then add enough of the remaining oil to make the consistency you prefer.

8 Arrange a few slices of fish on each plate with a portion of skordalia and garnish with wedges of lemon.

Serving suggestions This is a complete meal that needs no accompaniment, but you could offer a crisp green salad if you wish.

Mediterranean flavour Salt cod is common in Mediterranean and especially Spanish, Italian and Greek cooking, as it provides a way of preserving the fish through the winter.

Photograph opposite:
Veal Cakes with Mango Salsa and Spinach Salad (see page 58)

Grapefruit, avocado and prawn salad

The bigger the prawns the better for this dish, as they add colour and look really impressive. If you want to avoid arguments, count the number of prawns so that everyone can have the same amount!

SERVES 6

24 raw king prawns (jumbo shrimp), peeled and deveined

2 yellow grapefruit

2 ruby grapefruit

300 g/11 oz mixed salad leaves

1 red (bell) pepper, cut into julienne strips

1 yellow pepper, cut into julienne strips

1 red onion, thinly sliced

3 avocados

30 ml/2 tbsp lemon juice

FOR THE DRESSING

375 ml/13 fl oz/1½ cups Home-made Mayonnaise (see page 29)

120 ml/4 fl oz/½ cup tomato ketchup (catsup)

15–30 ml/1–2 tbsp Tabasco sauce

15 ml/1 tbsp Worcestershire sauce

30 ml/2 tbsp lemon or lime juice

Salt and freshly ground black pepper

A few whole chive stalks, to garnish

Photograph opposite:
Duck Breasts Marinated with Marmalade (see page 76)

1 Bring a large pan of water to the boil, add the prawns and boil for a couple of minutes, just until they turn pink. Do not overcook them. Drain and rinse under cold water to stop the cooking.

2 Pare away the peel and pith of the grapefruit, using a sharp knife. Hold the fruit over a large bowl to catch the juice and cut down the sides of each segment. Add the flesh to the bowl.

3 Add the salad leaves, peppers and red onion and toss gently. Arrange the salad mixture on individual plates.

4 Peel and stone (pit) the avocados, then halve them. Slice each half lengthways without cutting completely through at the top of the avocado so that you can fan out the pieces. Sprinkle with lemon juice to prevent them from browning, and place them on the plates at the side of the salad. Arrange the prawns over the top.

5 Beat the mayonnaise until smooth, then stir in the remaining dressing ingredients, seasoning well with salt and pepper.

6 Drizzle some of the dressing over the salad and garnish with a few chive stalks in the centre.

7 Serve with the remainder of the dressing offered separately.

Serving suggestions This is a fresh salad that can easily be used as a summer lunch or dinner meal.

Hints and variations This salad can also be served on a bed of salad leaves, or chop half the prawns and add them to some chopped iceberg lettuce and some of the dressing and top with the rest of the salad ingredients.

meat main courses

Red meats can often be of poor quality in the Mediterranean
markets and butchers – thin, chewy steaks or a morsel of meat
on a local lamb chop – so I find I use a lot of pork and veal.
However, with great yacht provisioners and the open European
borders, I can get top quality meats from all over the world, so
I have no worries now about serving juicy steaks and large
lamb chops.

Lamb fillets with couscous and vegetables

Lamb fillets are always tender and juicy and are a versatile cut of meat. You can also use lamb steaks or even chops. The fresh herbs, vegetables and harissa – a hot chilli paste from North Africa – make this a delightfully exotic dish.

SERVES 6

1 litre/1¾ pts/4¼ cups plain yoghurt

15 ml/1 tbsp chopped fresh rosemary

6 garlic cloves, finely chopped

About 120 ml/4 fl oz/1 cup olive oil

6 small lamb fillets

200 g/7 oz sweet potatoes, chopped into large dice

200 g/7 oz aubergines (eggplants), chopped into large dice

300 g/11 oz red and yellow (bell) peppers, chopped into large dice

400 g/14 oz cherry tomatoes

2 onions, chopped

A few sprigs of fresh thyme

A few sprigs of fresh oregano

1 chilli, seeded and chopped

225 g/8 oz/2 cups couscous

Salt and freshly ground black pepper

600 ml/1 pt/2½ cups hot vegetable stock

50 g/2 oz/1 cup chopped fresh mint

5 ml/1 tsp caster (superfine) sugar

5 ml/1 tsp harrisa

Juice of two lemons

15 ml/1 tbsp tomato purée (paste)

2.5 ml/1 tsp ground cumin

2.5 ml/1 tsp ground coriander (cilantro)

1 Line a metal sieve (strainer) with two layers of kitchen paper (paper towels), spoon in the yoghurt and allow this to drain. You may need to empty the bowl and change the kitchen paper.

2 Mix the rosemary and half the garlic with 30 ml/2 tbsp of the olive oil and rub over the lamb fillets. Set aside for 20 minutes. Preheat the oven 200°C/400°F/gas 6/fan oven 180°C.

3 Put the sweet potatoes in a saucepan, cover with water, bring to the boil and boil for 10 minutes. Drain well.

4 Mix the sweet potatoes with the aubergines, peppers, tomatoes and onions in a baking tin (pan) and toss in a little olive oil until coated. Add the thyme, oregano, chilli and remaining garlic. Place in the oven and cook for 30 minutes until cooked through and browned, turning twice.

5 Meanwhile, heat about 30 ml/2 tbsp of the olive oil in a large frying pan (skillet) and fry (sauté) the fillets for about 3 minutes on each side until sealed. Place in a baking tin and roast in the oven for 10 minutes.

6 To make the couscous, place it in a large bowl, stir in 45 ml/3 tbsp olive oil and season with salt and pepper. Pour the hot stock over the couscous, cover and leave to stand for about 5 minutes, then fluff it up with a fork. Adjust the seasoning to taste.

7 Place the yoghurt in a bowl and mix in the chopped mint and sugar.

8 Mix the harrisa, lemon juice, tomato purée, cumin and coriander in a separate bowl.

9 Spoon the couscous on to the plates and add the vegetables. Pour the harrisa mixture over. Slice the lamb fillets thickly, then place them on top and spoon on the minted yoghurt. Serve immediately.

Serving suggestions A tomato salad will provide a cool contrast to the spicy flavours in this dish.

Steaks on garlic mash with gorgonzola cream

This dish looks absolutely spectacular on a white serving plate and the flavours are just superb, with the Gorgonzola cream giving it an exciting bite! You can cook the beef for a longer or shorter time, depending on your taste.

SERVES 6–8

1 beef fillet, about 2 kg/4½ lb

2 kiwi fruit, sliced, with the skin left on

Salt and freshly ground black pepper

30 ml/2 tbsp made English mustard

30 ml/2 tbsp horseradish sauce

1 whole head of garlic

120 ml/4 fl oz/½ cup water

6 Roma tomatoes,
cut in half lengthways

250 ml/8 fl oz/1 cup olive oil

5 ml/1 tsp chopped fresh oregano

5 ml/1 tsp chopped fresh thyme

1 kg/2¼ lb baby leeks

700 g/1½ lb potatoes, peeled

100 g/4 oz Gorgonzola cheese

400 ml/14 fl oz/1¾ cups single
(light) cream

30 ml/2 tbsp dry vermouth

120 ml/4 fl oz/½ cup red wine

300 ml/½ pt/1¼ cups beef or
chicken stock

15 ml/1 tbsp plain (all-purpose) flour

15 ml/1 tbsp butter

120 ml/4 fl oz/½ cup milk (optional)

1 Cut the fillet into eight steaks, place a slice of kiwi fruit on each side of each steak and leave to tenderise for 15 minutes.

2 Season the steaks with salt and pepper, then rub with the mustard and horseradish. Leave to marinate for 30 minutes.

3 Preheat the oven to 200°C/400°F/gas 6/fan oven 180°C.

4 Put the whole head of garlic in a small ovenproof dish with the water, cover with foil and roast in the oven for 1 hour. Remove and allow to cool, then slip the cloves out of their skins.

5 Arrange the tomatoes in a baking tin (pan), drizzle with half the olive oil and season with the herbs and salt and pepper. Place in the oven and bake for about 1 hour until they are tender and slightly browned.

6 Blanch the leeks, toss in about 15 ml/1 tbsp of the remaining oil and roast in the oven until lightly browned. Alternatively, grill (broil) them until lightly charred.

7 Place the potatoes in a saucepan of salted water, bring to the boil and boil for about 30 minutes until soft enough to mash.

8 To make the Gorgonzola cream, melt the cheese with the cream and vermouth and bring to the boil. Season with pepper and leave to simmer until the sauce has reduced by about half.

9 Heat the a frying pan (skillet) and sear the steaks for 3 minutes on each side, then place in the oven for 5 minutes until they are cooked to your liking.

10 Pour the wine into the pan and blend with the meat juices to make a gravy. Add the stock and bring to the boil. Blend the flour and butter to make a roux, then whisk it into the pan to thicken the gravy. Season to taste with salt and pepper. Strain the gravy twice to give it a rich, shiny look.

11 Drain the potatoes and mash with the remaining olive oil and the roasted garlic. Season with salt and pepper and add milk as necessary to get the creaminess you like.

12 Spoon the potato on to warm plates and top with the steaks. Arrange the tomatoes and leeks around the edge, then spoon over the Gorgonzola cream and drizzle the gravy around the edge. Serve immediately.

Hints and variations The enzymes in kiwi fruit are great for tenderising meats, so I like to use them with beef, veal and lamb when I am not sure about the quality of the meat. You can substitute other vegetables, for instance asparagus instead of the leeks, or use steamed rice instead of the garlic mash.

Beef carpaccio with tomato, onion and cornichon salsa

Since carpaccio is a raw-meat dish, I only serve this when I know that the meat is extremely fresh. You need to cut the meat into wafer-thin slices, so make sure you have a really sharp knife.

SERVES 6–8

750 g/1¾ lb beef fillet, as fresh as possible

2 garlic cloves, finely chopped

6 tomatoes, seeded and finely chopped

1 red onion, finely chopped

3 cornichons, finely chopped

45 ml/3 tbsp olive oil

Freshly ground black pepper

1 Place the fillet in the freezer for 30 minutes so that it is firm enough for you to slice it very finely.

2 Take it out and cut into wafer-thin slices. Lay the pieces on a large, flat dish.

3 Mix together the remaining ingredients and pour over the meat. Serve immediately.

Serving suggestions All you need to accompany this delicious meat is lots of fresh crusty bread and butter.

Hints and variations Served with a salad, this is a great dish for a summer lunch as well as a good starter for a dinner menu.

Beef fillet salad with thai-style dressing

The Asian treatment works well here, and using beef adds an unusual dimension and flavour to a salad. You can easily vary the salad ingredients according to what you have available.

SERVES 8

15 ml/1 tbsp yellow mustard seeds

15 ml/1 tbsp finely chopped chilli

2 stalks of lemon grass, crushed

4 cm/1½ in piece of fresh root ginger, peeled and grated

2 garlic cloves, crushed

30 ml/2 tbsp sesame oil

120 ml/4 fl oz/½ cup lime juice

25 g/1 oz/½ cup chopped fresh mint

50 g/2 oz/1 cup chopped fresh coriander (cilantro)

50 g/2 oz/1 cup chopped spinach leaves

50 g/2 oz/1 cup chopped spring onions (scallions)

1 kg/2¼ lb beef fillet, cut into 5 mm/¼ in slices

300 g/11 oz mixed salad leaves

2 red onions, thinly sliced

1 red (bell) pepper, cut into julienne strips

1 yellow pepper, cut into julienne strips

4 carrots, cut into julienne strips

75 g/3 oz/½ cup grated fresh coconut

15 ml/1 tbsp sesame seeds

1 Crush the mustard seeds and mix together with the chilli, half the lemon grass, half the ginger, the garlic, half the sesame oil and 15 ml/1 tbsp of the lime juice in a food processor. Add the mint, coriander, spinach leaves and spring onions and process to a fine paste.

2 Pour over the beef slices and leave to marinate for at least 30 minutes.

3 Heat a heavy-based frying pan (skillet) or wok and fry (sauté) the meat over a high heat for a few minutes until just cooked to your liking.

4 Toss the salad leaves with the red onions, peppers, carrots and grated coconut.

5 Mix the remaining lemon grass, ginger, sesame oil and lime juice to make a dressing.

6 Mix the meat with the salad, pour over the dressing and toss everything. Sprinkle with the sesame seeds.

7 Serve in individual bowls.

Serving suggestion: I like to serve this with steamed rice, or on a bed of thick rice noodles. Or you can always have it with crusty bread.

Hints and variations You can also create a lighter version of this recipe using chicken or fish instead of beef.

Breaded veal with sautéed tomatoes

Veal is eaten extensively in Italy as the quality is excellent. One young Spanish boy I have cooked for ate nothing but breaded veal until I breaded some turkey breast, which works just as well in this recipe.

SERVES 6–8

60 ml/4 tbsp olive oil

4 garlic cloves, crushed

1½ kg/3 lb cherry tomatoes

3 eggs

120 ml/4 fl oz/½ cup milk

25 g/1 oz/½ cup chopped fresh parsley

Salt and freshly ground black pepper

250 ml/8 fl oz/1 cup water

45 ml/3 tbsp balsamic vinegar

6 veal escalopes, very thinly sliced

175 g/6 oz/1½ cups plain (all-purpose) flour

100 g/4 oz/2 cups fresh breadcrumbs

50 g/2 oz/1 cup chopped fresh basil

1 Preheat the oven to 200°C/400°F/gas 6/fan oven 180°C.

2 Heat half the olive oil in a large frying pan (skillet) and fry (sauté) the garlic for a minute, then add the tomatoes and stir well to coat the tomatoes in the oil. Cook gently for 20 minutes, stirring regularly but very gently in order to keep the tomatoes as whole as you can.

3 Meanwhile, beat together the eggs and milk, then stir in the parsley and season with salt and pepper.

4 Add the water and balsamic vinegar to the tomatoes and continue to cook for a further 10 minutes while you cook the veal.

5 Heat the remaining oil in a large frying pan (skillet). Coat the veal in the flour, then in the egg mixture, and then dredge in breadcrumbs. Cook in the pan for about 3 minutes on each side until golden.

6 Season the tomatoes with salt and pepper and add the basil.

7 Put the veal in a large serving dish and pour the cherry tomatoes over. Sprinkle generously with basil and serve.

Serving suggestions A side platter of roasted potatoes and a fresh salad makes a good accompaniment.

Veal in wine and thyme sauce with puff pastry caps

If you're making this dish for children, try making the dish look more fun by decorating the caps with leaves or animal shapes made of pastry! Simply use their favourite biscuit (cookie) cutter.

SERVES 6–8

500 g/18 oz/1 large packet of puff pastry (paste)

A little milk

45 ml/3 tbsp olive oil

2 onions, chopped

6 garlic cloves, crushed

450 g/1 lb button mushrooms

1½ kg/3 lb veal fillet, diced

75 g/3 oz/¾ cups plain (all-purpose) flour

5 sprigs of fresh thyme

300 ml/½ pt/1¼ cups chicken stock

300 ml/½ pt/1¼ cups dry white wine

Salt and freshly ground black pepper

30 ml/2 tbsp butter or margarine, softened

1 Roll out the pastry, cut into 8 or 16 squares, lay on a greased baking (cookie) sheet and brush with the milk. Chill for 30 minutes while you prepare the veal.

2 Heat half the olive oil in a frying pan (skillet) and sauté the onions and garlic for a few minutes until softened but not browned. Add the mushrooms and cook for 10 minutes until soft. Remove from the pan.

3 Heat the remaining olive oil in the pan. Toss the veal in 50 g/2 oz/ ½ cup of the flour, then sauté in the pan for a few minutes until lightly browned. Add the thyme, reserving one sprig for garnish, return the mushrooms and onions to the pan and stir together.

4 Add half the stock and half the wine and bring to the boil, stirring all the time to create a light sauce without any lumps. Gradually add the remaining stock and wine, bring to a simmer and cook gently for 20 minutes until the veal is cooked through and tender, stirring regularly. Season to taste with salt and pepper.

5 Preheat the oven to 180°C/350°F/gas 4/fan oven 160°C. Score the surface of the pastry to decorate and bake in the oven for 10–15 minutes until risen and golden. Remove from the oven and set aside.

6 Remove the thyme sprigs from the pan. Mix the remaining flour with the butter or margarine to make a roux, then gradually whisk in a spoonful at a time until the sauce has thickened to your preferred consistency.

7 Arrange the veal and mushrooms on plates with a square of puff pastry on the top and add a little colour by garnishing each one with a few leaves from the reserved sprig of fresh thyme.

Serving suggestion Serve with a mixed salad.

Hints and variations The sauce goes extremely well with chicken too so, if you don't want to eat red meats, you could substitute chicken breasts for the veal.

Veal cakes with mango salsa and spinach salad

*This dish steals a little from the Caribbean with its delicious sweet mango salsa,
spiced with a hint of chilli. The spinach makes a wonderful contrast of colours
and flavours. See photograph opposite page 48.*

SERVES 6–8

FOR THE CAKES

700 g/1½ lb minced (ground) veal

2 red chillies, finely chopped

1 white onion, chopped

**1 bunch of spring onions
(scallions), chopped**

**50 g/2 oz/1 cup chopped fresh
coriander (cilantro)**

50 g/2 oz/1 cup chopped fresh parsley

**2.5 cm/1 in piece of fresh root ginger,
peeled and grated**

Grated zest of 1 lemon

1 egg, beaten

Flour for dusting

Olive oil for shallow-frying

**Spinach Salad with Ginger Dressing
(see opposite)**

FOR THE MANGO SALSA

**4 mangos, peeled, stoned (pitted)
and finely diced**

6 spring onions, finely chopped

**50 g/2 oz/1 cup roughly chopped
fresh coriander**

1 red chilli, seeded and finely chopped

½ cucumber, seeded and diced

1 To make the veal cakes, put the veal, chillies, onions, coriander, parsley, ginger and lemon in a bowl and mix together. Add the egg to bind. Form 24 small cakes, cover and chill for 1 hour.

2 Mix together all the ingredients for the mango salsa, cover and chill until ready to use.

3 Dust the veal cakes in flour. Heat the oil in a heavy-based frying pan (skillet) and sauté the veal cakes a few minutes on each side until golden, then reduce the heat and continue to cook for about 15 minutes until cooked through.

4 Meanwhile, make up the Spinach Salad with Ginger Dressing.

5 Arrange the veal cakes on a bed of the salad and serve with the salsa on the side.

Serving suggestions I sometimes deep-fry some rice noodles to sprinkle on the top.

Hints and variations You can substitute chicken for the veal if you prefer. The salsa can be served with all kinds of dishes, especially Thai fish cakes or chicken dishes.

Spinach salad with ginger dressing

Baby spinach leaves make an excellent salad and are complemented perfectly by the tangy ingredients in the ginger dressing. If any of the leaves have a thick stem, simply pull it off.

SERVES 6–8

FOR THE SALAD

300 g/11 oz baby spinach leaves

1 red onion, thinly sliced

1 red (bell) pepper, cut into julienne strips

½ cucumber, cut into julienne strips

50 g/2 oz/1 cup chopped fresh mint leaves

50 g/2 oz/½ cup sesame seeds

FOR THE GINGER DRESSING

4 cm/1½ in piece of fresh root ginger, peeled and grated

5 ml/1 tsp soy sauce

30 ml/2 tbsp olive oil

15 ml/1 tbsp balsamic vinegar

1 Prepare all the salad ingredients and mix together.

2 Whisk together the dressing ingredients.

3 Just before serving, pour over the salad and toss together. Serve immediately.

Serving suggestions As well as being the perfect accompaniment for my Veal Cakes (see opposite), this is good enough to eat on its own or to be used as a side salad on just about any occasion.

Pork in garlic, chilli and capers with vermouth sauce

The cream and white wine make this a wonderful, succulent dish, but be careful not to overcook the pork as it does dry out quickly in the oven. Keep an eye on it and baste it from time to time.

SERVES 6–8

1½ kg/3 lb pork fillet

Salt and freshly ground black pepper

4 garlic cloves, crushed

2 fresh green chillies, seeded and finely chopped

50 g/2 oz/½ cup capers, rinsed and chopped

120 ml/4 fl oz/½ cup dry white wine or dry vermouth

1 kg/2¼ lb potatoes, peeled and cut into 5 mm/¼ in slices

120 ml/4 fl oz/½ cup olive oil

120 ml/4 fl oz/½ cup water

120 ml/4 fl oz/½ cup double (heavy) cream

1 Preheat the oven to 180°C/350°F/gas 4/fan oven 160°C.

2 Season the pork with salt and pepper. Heat a heavy-based frying pan (skillet) and sear the pork on both sides, then place it in a flameproof and ovenproof dish and add the garlic, chillies, capers and wine or vermouth.

3 Cook in the oven for 40 minutes, basting at least once during the cooking time.

4 Place the potato slices in a bowl and toss with the olive oil and salt and pepper. Arrange them in a baking (cookie) tray in overlapping rows (like fallen dominoes) and place in the oven.

5 Add the water to the pork and cover the dish with foil. Cook the potatoes and the pork for a further 50 minutes until the pork is tender and the potatoes are cooked through and golden.

6 Remove the pork from the oven and leave to rest for at least 10 minutes (this will make it easier to cut). Transfer to a warm serving dish and keep warm until you are ready to slice it.

7 Stir the cream into the pan of pork cooking juices. Cook over a low heat and stir gently until the sauce thickens.

8 Cut the pork into thick slices and arrange on a platter with the potatoes to one side. Pour over the sauce to serve.

Serving suggestions Instead of the crispy potato slices, I sometimes like to serve this with dauphinoise potatoes and a mixed salad or some grilled (broiled) or lightly steamed vegetables.

Prune-stuffed pork chops in a port jus

The flavour of these pork chops is reminiscent of North Africa or the eastern Mediterranean. Arabic cooking loves to combine sweet flavours with meat and almonds.

SERVES 6–8

16 ready-to-eat prunes

2 garlic cloves, crushed

50 g/2 oz/1 cup chopped fresh parsley

Salt and freshly ground black pepper

1 egg, beaten

50 g/2 oz/¹/₂ cup chopped almonds

6 thick pork chops

300 ml/¹/₂ pt/1¹/₄ cups chicken stock

100 ml/3¹/₂ fl oz/scant ¹/₂ cup port

30 ml/2 tbsp butter

30 ml/2 tbsp olive oil

225 g/8 oz/2 cups plain (all-purpose) flour

450 ml/³/₄ pt/2 cups milk

100 g/4 oz/2 cups fresh breadcrumbs

1 Place half the prunes, the garlic and the parsley in a blender and pulse until the prunes are very finely chopped. Season well with salt and pepper and add the beaten egg and chopped almonds.

2 Cut a pocket in the side of each pork chop and stuff with the prune mixture.

3 Slice the remaining prunes in half and set aside.

4 Bring the stock and port to the boil in a small pan, then boil until reduced by half. Rub the sauce twice through a sieve (strainer), then reheat. Stir in the reserved prunes.

5 Heat the butter and olive oil in a heavy-based frying pan (skillet). Dip the pork chops in the flour, then the milk and finally the breadcrumbs to coat completely. Gently fry (sauté) the chops for about 20 minutes, turning, until cooked through and golden on both sides.

6 Arrange the chops on warm plates and pour the jus around, then serve.

Serving suggestions These pork chops can be presented on a bed of mashed sweet potato or parsnip or onion mash. I think the richness of the jus is best complemented by simple steamed or grilled (broiled) vegetables or a tossed salad.

Hints and variations If you want to thicken the sauce a little further, blend 15 ml/1 tbsp butter and 15 ml/1 tbsp flour to make a roux. Whisk it into the reduced sauce a little at a time at step 4 until it is the thickness you like. Then rub through the sieve as above.

Roasted pork souvlaki with tzatziki

You can cook the meat and make the tzatziki in advance and the rest of the dish is simplicity itself, so this makes a great snack or light lunch, especially when we are on the go and cruising around.

SERVES 6–8

1½ kg/3 lb pork fillet

5 ml/1 tsp dried thyme

5 ml/1 tsp dried oregano

Salt and freshly ground black pepper

60 ml/4 tbsp olive oil

120 ml/4 fl oz/½ cup white wine

250 ml/8 fl oz/1 cup chicken or vegetable stock

12 tortillas

2 red onions, finely chopped

100 g/4 oz/2 cups roughly chopped fresh parsley

1 quantity of Tzatziki (see page 11)

6 tomatoes, roughly sliced

1 cos lettuce, shredded

Wedges of lemon, to garnish

1 Preheat the oven to 180°C/350°F/gas 4/fan oven 160°C.

2 Rub the pork fillet with the herbs, salt and pepper. Heat the oil in a frying pan (skillet) and sear the pork on all sides until it is brown.

3 Place the fillet in an ovenproof dish, pour over the wine and stock and cook in the oven for 20 minutes. Cover with foil, then cook for a further 25 minutes. Remove from the oven, leave to cool, then slice into strips.

4 Warm the tortillas in the oven.

5 Mix together the onion and parsley.

6 Spread each tortilla with tzatziki, then add some strips of pork, a slice or two of tomato, a spoonful of the onion mixture and finally some shredded lettuce. Season to taste with salt and pepper, then roll up the tortilla around the filling.

7 Arrange the wraps on a platter, garnish with wedges of lemon and serve.

Serving suggestions I like to offer a big bowl of fresh tomato salad or a mixed green salad with these.

Hints and variations You can use warm pitta breads instead of tortillas if you prefer. Just slit along one side and open up to form a pocket, then fill with all the ingredients as before.

I tend to use flatleaf parsley as it is so readily available throughout the Mediterranean.

Pork escalopes with sage and cheese

In the Mediterranean you can buy pork escalopes cut from the pork loin; they are just the right thickness – not too thin or too thick. I use these pieces quite a lot in my cooking as they can be cooked in many different ways.

SERVES 6

6 pork escalopes

150 g/5 oz Emmental (Swiss) cheese, sliced

12 sage leaves

100 g/4 oz Gorgonzola cheese, sliced

Salt and freshly ground black pepper

45 ml/3 tbsp olive oil

175 g/6 oz/1½ cups plain (all-purpose) flour

2 eggs, beaten

175 g/6 oz/3 cups fresh breadcrumbs

120 ml/4 fl oz/½ cup dry white wine

120 ml/4 fl oz/½ cup chicken stock

1 Preheat the oven to 180°C/350°F/gas 4/fan oven 160°C.

2 Flatten the escalopes with a meat mallet or rolling pin until they are very thin. Lay a piece of the Swiss cheese on each escalope, then 2 sage leaves and a small slice of Gorgonzola. Roll up the pork and secure it with either a cocktail stick (toothpick) or cook's string. Season well with salt and pepper.

3 Heat the oil in a heavy-based frying pan (skillet). Dip the pork in the flour, then in the beaten egg, then in the breadcrumbs, and gently fry (sauté) for about 5 minutes on each side until golden brown.

4 Transfer to an ovenproof dish and bake in the oven for a further 10 minutes.

5 Pour the wine and stock into the frying pan and bring to the boil, scraping up any meat juices and sediment in the pan to make a light sauce. Boil gently to allow it to reduce and thicken.

6 Slice the pork escalopes into three or four pieces. Arrange on warm plates, pour the gravy over and serve immediately.

Serving suggestions These go well with roasted potatoes and grilled (broiled) vegetables.

Hints and variations The escalopes can be cooked without being braised. Sear them in a hot pan until lightly browned, then cook for 10 minutes in the oven as above.

Peppercorn pork salad with bananas

This delicious salad has a slightly exotic flavour, with the sweetness of the pineapple and banana bringing in an Asian feel to the dish, combined with the coconut milk and chilli.

SERVES 6–8

30 ml/2 tbsp sezchuan peppercorns, crushed

1½ kg/3 lb pork fillet

30 ml/2 tbsp olive oil

100 g/4 oz/1 cup peanuts

300 g/11 oz mixed salad leaves

2 white onions, sliced

1 punnet of mustard and cress

½ fresh pineapple, sliced

4 firm ripe bananas

FOR THE DRESSING

200 ml/7 fl oz/1 small can of coconut milk

4 cm/1½ in piece of fresh root ginger, grated

50 g/2 oz/1 cup finely chopped fresh coriander (cilantro)

1 red chilli, seeded and thinly sliced

15 ml/1 tbsp lime juice

1 Preheat the oven to 180°C/350°F/gas 4/fan oven 160°C.

2 Rub the peppercorns into the pork. Heat the oil in a frying pan (skillet) and sear the pork for a few minutes to seal on all sides, then transfer to an ovenproof dish and place in the oven for about 35 minutes until cooked through. Allow to cool, then cut into thin slices.

3 Toast the peanuts in a dry frying pan for a few minutes until golden.

4 Toss the salad leaves with the onion and mustard and cress. Arrange on the plates with the slices of pineapple. Finely slice the bananas at an angle and arrange on the salad, then top with the pork.

5 Mix together the dressing ingredients and shake well.

6 When ready to serve, pour the dressing over the pork and salad and sprinkle with the peanuts.

7 Serve in individual bowls.

Serving suggestions This is a meal in itself, but you could accompany it with some crisp ciabatta or warmed pitta breads. Offer the rest of the dressing in a jug to be passed around the table.

Hints and variations The salad can also be made with poached or grilled (broiled) chicken or turkey, or a white, firm-fleshed fish that has been lightly grilled or pan fried (sautéed).

Squash gnocchi with a sage sauce and crispy bacon

These gnocchi are quite filling, and serving them with the sage sauce and crispy bacon makes a delicious and very satisfying meal.

SERVES 6–8

200 g/7 oz/scant 1 cup butter

1 kg/2¼ lb butternut squash, halved and seeded

Salt and freshly ground black pepper

100 g/4 oz/1 cup freshly grated Parmesan cheese

100 g/4 oz/1 cup freshly grated Gruyère (Swiss) cheese

225 g/8 oz/2 cups plain (all-purpose) flour, plus extra for dusting

200 g/7 oz bacon pieces, crisped

8 sage leaves, finely chopped

1 Preheat the oven to 180°C/350°F/gas 4/fan oven 160°C.

2 Place a little of the butter in each squash half and season well with salt and pepper. Place in a baking tin (pan) and roast in the oven for 45 minutes until soft.

3 Remove the flesh from the skin. Mash the flesh and place it in a sieve (strainer) over a bowl. Cover with a plate and top with a weight to press it down and drain off any juices.

4 Transfer the squash flesh to a bowl, add the cheeses and season with salt and pepper. The mixture will be quite damp, so gradually add enough of the flour, a little at a time, to form a fairly stiff dough. Cover the bowl and chill in the fridge for 1 hour.

5 Shape the chilled mixture into walnut-sized balls and dust with flour.

6 Bring a large pan of salted water to the boil. Add a few gnocchi at a time and boil gently until they float back up to the surface. Remove with a slotted spoon and drain well, then place in an ovenproof dish in the oven. Repeat until you have cooked all the gnocchi.

7 Meanwhile, fry (sauté) the bacon pieces in a frying pan (skillet) for about 10 minutes until crisp, then remove from the pan and drain off the fat. Add the remaining butter to the pan with the sage and plenty of black pepper. Return the bacon to the pan.

8 When all the gnocchi are cooked, pour over the sage sauce, top with the crispy bacon and serve at once.

Serving suggestions A large bowl of fresh salad leaves is all you need to serve with this dish.

Hints and variations Try to handle the gnocchi as little as possible otherwise they will become rather heavy.

Onion pancakes with radicchio, bacon and roasted peppers

A great dish for summer lunch, these are light and tasty but substantial enough to satisfy hearty appetites. The quantity of dressing is large, but it is very popular and any leftovers can be stored in the fridge.

SERVES 6–8

4 eggs

900 ml/1½ pts/3¾ cups milk

450 g/1 lb/4 cups plain (all-purpose) flour

25 g/1 oz/2 tbsp butter, melted

Salt and freshly ground black pepper

100 g/4 oz/2 cups chopped fresh parsley

2 bunches of spring onions (scallions), chopped

10 ml/2 tsp baking powder

50 g/2 oz/¼ cup butter

FOR THE FILLING

400 g/14 oz bacon, chopped

3 radicchio lettuces, roughly chopped

1 bunch of rocket, roughly chopped

4 (bell) peppers, roasted and diced

50 g/2 oz/½ cup freshly grated Parmesan cheese

1 Whisk together the eggs and milk, then whisk in the flour and melted butter and season with salt and pepper. Set aside to stand for 30 minutes.

2 Mix in the parsley and spring onions, then add the baking powder.

3 Melt a little of the butter in a small crêpe pan, then pour in a small amount of batter and tip the pan so that it coats the whole base. Cook on one side until bubbles appear to burst on the top, then gently turn it over and cook for a few minutes on the other side. Transfer to an ovenproof dish, cover with foil and keep warm in the oven while you make the remaining pancakes in the same way.

4 To make the filling, fry (sauté) the chopped bacon for about 10 minutes until golden, then remove from the pan. Drain off and reserve as much of the juices as you can. Mix the radicchio and rocket into the bacon.

5 Whisk together all the ingredients for the balsamic dressing.

6 Lay a pancake on each plate and spoon on some of the bacon salad, add some diced pepper, then 5 ml/1 tsp of the Parmesan. Top with another pancake and then spoon over some of the bacon juices.

7 Serve drizzled with a little balsamic dressing.

FOR THE BALSAMIC DRESSING

300 ml/¹/₂ pt/1¹/₄ cups olive oil

150 ml/¹/₄ pt/²/₃ cup balsamic vinegar

15 ml/1 tbsp wholegrain mustard

30 ml/2 tbsp clear honey

15 ml/1 tbsp chopped garlic

10 ml/2 tsp fresh mixed herbs

Salt and freshly ground black pepper

Serving suggestions These pancakes are a delicious meal in themselves, but you could accompany them with a tomato salad.

Hints and variations I use this recipe to make tiny blini-type crêpes that can be topped with soured (dairy sour) cream and chives or caviare. I also like to add texture to the batter by mixing in julienned carrots or courgettes (zucchini) with mint, sweetcorn (corn) and parsley. You can vary the filling too – use chicken or fish instead of bacon, or fill the pancakes with a tossed salad of mixed leaves, sun-blush tomatoes and Feta cheese.

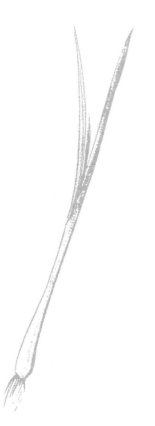

poultry main courses

I use a lot of chicken in my cooking as it is low in fat, readily available and so versatile. Chicken breasts are a cook's dream – you can stuff them, slice them into fillets, dice them for kebabs, mince (grind) the meat or just use them whole. Turkey breasts can be used instead of chicken for more variety. They contain less fat than chicken but tend to dry out more so need to be basted or watched carefully. Whole roasted chicken is a popular meal with my guests, and I also like to use poussin (Cornish hen), duck and quail. There is something special about presenting a whole poussin for each guest on a special occasion.

Marinated chicken kebabs

These kebabs can be cooked in a hot oven, but grilling gives a great colour to the meat so I prefer to cook the chicken that way. Remember to soak your skewers in cold water for at least 30 minutes so that they do not burn when cooking.

SERVES 6

30 ml/2 tbsp coriander (cilantro) seeds

30 ml/2 tbsp cumin seeds

30 ml/2 tbsp fenugreek seeds

30 ml/2 tbsp cardamom seeds

450 ml/³/₄ pt/2 cups plain yoghurt

6 chicken breasts, diced

5 onions, cut into chunks

3 red or yellow (bell) peppers, cut into 2.5 cm/1 in squares

Salt and freshly ground black pepper

Juice of ½ lemon

1 Dry-roast all the seeds in a frying pan (skillet) for a few minutes, shaking the pan until they are golden. Grind them in a pestle and mortar, then stir into the yoghurt.

2 Add the chicken to the yoghurt marinade, cover and leave to marinate in the fridge for at least 1 hour, or longer if you want a stronger flavour.

3 Thread the meat on to soaked wooden skewers, alternating with the onion and pepper. Season with salt and pepper and squeeze over the lemon juice.

4 Grill (broil) or barbecue the kebabs for about 20 minutes, turning regularly until cooked through and lightly browned.

5 Serve immediately.

Serving suggestions Serve the kebabs with a bowl of plain boiled rice and a tossed salad.

Hints and variations You could also use this with a firm, white-fleshed fish such swordfish – I sometimes use wahoo, but I don't think you'll find that in your local supermarket!

Mediterranean flavour Whenever we dock in a new port, I love to search out the local shops. Once you leave the immediate dock area, you often find the most wonderful streets full of great food shops of all description. The best have butchers, delicatessens, patisseries, bread shops, fresh pasta shops and fruit and vegetable shops plus little stalls along the road selling fresh local fruit and vegetables.

Rolled chicken breast fillets with prosciutto

This dish is so easy to prepare and the basil, prosciutto and vermouth give you a really authentic Mediterranean flavour. It also has a wonderful, bright combination of Italian colours.

SERVES 6

1 bunch of spring onions (scallions)

6 chicken breast fillets, flattened

225 g/8 oz/2 cups full-fat
soft cream cheese

12 baby spinach leaves

1 yellow (bell) pepper, thinly sliced

6 sun-dried tomatoes, sliced

6 fresh basil leaves

6 slices of Swiss cheese

6 slices of prosciutto

Salt and freshly ground black pepper

300 ml/½ pt/1¼ cups vermouth
or dry white wine

120 ml/4 fl oz/½ cup double
(heavy) cream

1 Preheat the oven to 200°C/400°F/gas 6/fan oven 180°C. Chop the spring onions into 3 cm/1¼ in length, then slice the pieces lengthways.

2 Lay the chicken breasts on a work surface and spread with the cream cheese, then cover with the spinach. Top each one with some spring onions, pepper, sun-dried tomatoes and a basil leaf and finish with a slice of Swiss cheese. Roll up the fillets, wrap each one with a slice of prosciutto and secure with cocktail sticks (toothpicks).

3 Arrange the rolls in a single layer in an oiled flameproof, ovenproof dish, season with salt and pepper and pour over the vermouth or wine. Cover and cook in the oven for 30 minutes until the chicken is cooked through. The cooking time will vary depending on the size of the rolls.

4 Transfer the chicken rolls to the grill (broiler) and grill (broil) for a few minutes to brown the top.

5 Meanwhile, pour the cream into the cooking juices and warm through gently, stirring to make a creamy sauce.

6 Slice the stuffed rolls. Arrange the pieces, fanned out, on warm plates, and serve with a little of the sauce poured around.

Serving suggestions Crispy roasted potatoes and steamed vegetables go down well with this dish.

Hints and variations You can use either chicken or turkey breast fillets with this recipe – I prefer chicken as it seems to remain moist in the oven. You can also use other ingredients for the filling if you wish. Try asparagus instead of the pepper, or just fill the rolls with a mixture of ricotta cheese and chopped spinach.

Exotic chicken salad

Poached chicken stays beautifully moist, making it perfect for serving cold. The nuts and pineapple curry sauce give a really exotic flavour to this salad, making it great for all occasions.

SERVES 6

250 ml/8 fl oz/1 cup plain yoghurt

6 chicken breasts

1 carrot

1 onion, halved

1 celery stick

1 bay leaf

250 ml/8 fl oz/1 cup mayonnaise

50 g/2 oz/½ cup mango chutney

30 ml/2 tbsp tomato ketchup (catsup)

Salt and freshly ground black pepper

120 ml/4 fl oz/½ cup pineapple juice

1 fresh pineapple, peeled and diced

450 g/1 lb green grapes, halved and seeded if necessary

100 g/4 oz/1 cup flaked (slivered) almonds

1 Place the yoghurt in a sieve (strainer) lined with a piece of clean muslin (cheesecloth) and leave to drain for 1 hour.

2 Place the chicken breasts in a large saucepan with the carrot, onion, celery stick and bay leaf and bring to the boil. Reduce the heat and simmer gently for about 20 minutes until the chicken is cooked through. Allow to cool slightly in the stock, then remove, cut into dice and leave to cool thoroughly. Discard the vegetables.

3 Mix the mayonnaise with the drained yoghurt. Stir in the mango chutney and tomato ketchup. Season well with salt and pepper, then stir in the pineapple juice.

4 Add the pineapple and grapes, then stir in the chicken pieces and mix well.

5 Cover and chill for 30 minutes.

6 Lightly toast the almonds in a dry frying pan (skillet) until golden, shaking the pan all the time to prevent burning.

7 Arrange the chicken salad on a large platter and sprinkle with the toasted almonds, then serve.

Serving suggestions A light green salad is the perfect accompaniment to this dish.

Hints and variations You could use turkey breast or leg, or for a real change try it with prawns (shrimp) or lobster meat. Remember though, if you do use this sauce with seafood you need something with a fairly robust flavour. If you can't get fresh pineapple, just use fruit canned in natural juice and drain the pieces well. You could try melon instead of grapes, too.

Chicken satay with pineapple and peanut sauce

These are very simple to make and always very popular with children! You can offer a choice of sauces if you wish. Peanut sauce is the traditional Asian sauce but kids love tomato sauce, which you can always jazz up with a little chilli.

SERVES 6–8

250 ml/8 fl oz/1 cup soy sauce

4 garlic cloves, crushed

30 ml/2 tbsp sweet chilli sauce

6 chicken breasts, diced

350 g/12 oz/1½ cups peanut butter

400 ml/14 fl oz/1 large can of coconut milk

250 ml/8 fl oz/1 cup pineapple juice

120 ml/4 fl oz/½ cup whipping cream

15 ml/1 tbsp chilli paste

50 g/2 oz/1 cup chopped fresh coriander (cilantro)

1 Mix the soy sauce, garlic and chilli sauce. Pour over the chicken and leave to marinate for 30 minutes.

2 Thread the chicken on to soaked wooden skewers, then arrange in a grill (broiler) pan.

3 Grill (broil) the chicken for about 20 minutes, turning regularly, until cooked through and browned on all sides.

4 Very gently heat the peanut butter with the coconut milk and pineapple juice. Do not let it boil as it easily separates. If this does happen, remove from the heat and whisk in a little of the cream.

5 Just before serving, stir in the cream, chilli paste and coriander.

6 Put the skewers of chicken on warm plates and spoon the sauce over before serving.

Serving suggestions I like to arrange the satay sticks on a bed of boiled basmati or jasmine rice. Serve with a tossed green salad.

Hints and variations I have used peanut butter here to make the recipe easier, but I quite often make the peanut flavouring by grinding roasted peanuts with chillies to make a spicier dish. The chicken can be cut into smaller pieces and skewered on to cocktail sticks (toothpicks) and served as a canapé at a cocktail party. Again, don't forget to soak your skewers before you start.

Thai green curry with chicken and prawns

So full of colour and flavour, this is one of Thailand's simplest meals and one that always goes down well in the Mediterranean sunshine – although it's not strictly authentic! Try to buy coriander with the roots still attached, if possible.

SERVES 6–8

1 large bunch of fresh coriander (cilantro), thoroughly washed

45 ml/3 tbsp olive oil

2 garlic cloves, crushed

4 cm/1½ in piece of fresh root ginger, peeled and grated

30 ml/2 tbsp Thai green curry paste

1 red chilli, seeded and thinly sliced

300 ml/½ pt/1¼ cups coconut milk

3 chicken breasts, sliced into three strips

12 medium-sized raw prawns (shrimp), peeled and deveined

2 onions, sliced

12 baby corn cobs

1 red (bell) pepper, sliced lengthways

1 yellow pepper, sliced lengthways

1 orange pepper, sliced lengthways

200 g/7 oz mangetout (snow peas)

1 bunch of spring onions (scallions), chopped

1 Take a few stalks of coriander with all the roots out of the bunch and tie them together. Finely chop the rest of the bunch and set aside.

2 Heat half the oil in a frying pan (skillet) and fry (sauté) the garlic and ginger for a few minutes until aromatic. Add the curry paste, then the bundle of coriander stalks and roots and the chilli, then pour in the coconut milk and bring to the boil. Simmer gently for 5 minutes.

3 Meanwhile, heat the remaining oil in a clean frying pan and sear the chicken pieces, then remove them from the pan. Add the prawns and fry for a minute until just pink, then add to the chicken. Add the onions, baby corn and peppers to the pan and fry for 5 minutes, then add the mangetout and cook for a few minutes until all the vegetables are just tender but still crisp. Return the chicken and prawns to the pan.

4 Remove the coriander stalks from the sauce, then pour the sauce over the chicken and vegetables. Heat through, then stir in most of the reserved chopped coriander and the spring onions.

5 Serve on warm plates, garnished with the remainder of the chopped coriander.

Serving suggestions Steamed basmati or jasmine rice both go really well with this dish. You can present the curry with the rice on the side or, for a special touch, press the rice into ramekins (custard cups) and turn out a mound on each plate. Serve the curry spooned around the mound with lots of fresh chopped coriander scattered over the top.

Golden chicken breasts with tomatoes, pesto and mozzarella

Sun-dried tomatoes, pesto and Mozzarella – tastes that everyone associates with Italy – are all combined in this simple but delicious recipe. It is quick and easy to make too.

SERVES 6

6 chicken breasts

6 slices of Mozzarella cheese

6 sun-dried tomatoes, cut into halves

25 ml/1½ tbsp pesto sauce

100 g/4 oz/1 cup almonds, chopped

100 g/4 oz/2 cups fresh breadcrumbs

110 g/4 oz/1 cup plain (all-purpose) flour

4 eggs, beaten

1 Pierce the thick end of each chicken breast with a small sharp knife, then cut along into the middle of the breast to make a pocket.

2 Lay a piece of Mozzarella on top of a sun-dried tomato half, top with 2.5 ml/½ tsp of the pesto, then another sun-dried tomato half. Slide this into the hole you have pierced in the chicken and push it well inside. Repeat with the remaining breasts.

3 Mix together the chopped almonds and breadcrumbs. Dip the chicken into the flour, then the egg, then into the breadcrumb mixture. Chill for 30 minutes.

4 Preheat the oven to 180°C/350°F/gas 4/fan oven 160°C.

5 Cook the chicken breasts in the oven for 20 minutes until cooked through and tender.

6 Serve on warm plates.

Serving suggestions All you need is a fresh salad to serve with this dish, but you could also accompany it with pasta or rice if you like, or you can place each breast on top of a bed of mashed potatoes.

Hints and variations There are so many alternatives to this versatile dish. You can stuff the chicken breasts with pesto or sun-dried tomato, fried (sautéed) mushrooms, or even that old favourite, garlic and parsley. Play around and experiment to find what you like.

Mediterranean flavour In the wonderful Italian market town of Gaeta, I found two shops that sold fresh Mozzarella from huge vats full of brine and whey that came from Naples every day. At 3 o'clock in the afternoon, there was always a line of women waiting outside for the Mozzarella to arrive.

Chicken noodle salad

Colourful and tasty, this salad can be used at lunch or for a summer dinner. You can use whatever vegetables you like but make sure they are blanched before you make the salad so they are only lightly cooked.

SERVES 6–8

30 ml/2 tbsp sesame oil

60 ml/4 tbsp sweet chilli sauce

30 ml/2 tbsp mango chutney

4 chicken breasts, diced

200 g/7 oz French (green) beans, sliced

3 carrots, cut into julienne strips

200 g/7 oz mangetout (snow peas)

200 g/7 oz broccoli, cut into small florets

1 bunch of fresh coriander (cilantro)

½ bunch of fresh mint

2 red onions, sliced

6 garlic cloves, crushed

4 cm/1½ in piece of fresh root ginger, peeled and grated

4 courgettes (zucchini), cut into julienne strips

1 red or orange (bell) pepper, cut into julienne strips

1 green pepper, cut into julienne strips

375 g/13 oz/6 slabs of egg noodles

30 ml/2 tbsp soy sauce

120 ml/4 fl oz/½ cup lime juice

50 g/2 oz/½ cup sesame seeds

1 Heat half the sesame oil with half the sweet chilli sauce and the mango chutney. Toss the chicken into the saucepan and gently cook for about 15 minutes until tender. Set aside.

2 Bring a large pan of water to the boil. Add the beans, carrots, mangetout and broccoli, return to the boil, then drain and refresh in iced water to prevent them from cooking further and to keep the bright colours.

3 Chop half of the coriander; remove the leaves from the remaining half and set aside. Do the same with the mint.

4 Heat the remaining sesame oil in a frying pan (skillet) and fry (sauté) the onions, garlic and ginger for a few minutes until soft. Add the courgettes and peppers and cook for a few minutes until tender but still crisp.

5 Meanwhile, bring another pan of water to the boil, add the noodles and boil for about 4 minutes or according to the instructions on the packet. Drain, then plunge into iced water and drain again.

6 Whisk together the soy sauce, the remaining sweet chilli sauce and the lime juice, then pour over the noodles and toss well. Add the chicken and vegetables, chopped coriander and mint and toss again.

7 Arrange the chicken mixture on plates and dress with the sesame seeds and the reserved coriander and mint leaves.

Serving suggestions You can accompany this salad with crusty bread to make it even more filling. Scatter some sliced spring onions (scallions) over the noodles as a garnish, if you like.

Duck breasts marinated with marmalade

Duck holds a great deal of fat in its skin so you do not need to use any fat when you are cooking it. Fan-slicing the duck makes it look superb when you serve it, and the rich, colourful sauce perfectly complements its flavour. See photograph opposite page 49

SERVES 6

6 small duck breasts, skin left on

450 g/1 lb/1 jar of orange marmalade

500 ml/17 fl oz/2¼ cups fresh orange juice

120 ml/4 fl oz/½ cup port

Salt and freshly ground black pepper

120 ml/4 fl oz/½ cup chicken stock (optional)

450 g/1 lb/2 cups long-grain rice

900 ml/1½ pts/3¾ cups water

15 ml/1 tbsp olive oil

1 Preheat the oven to 200°C/400°F/gas 6/fan oven 180°C.

2 Flatten the duck breasts slightly using a rolling pin, then make diagonal slashes across the skin. This will not only help with cooking but will also stop the skin shrinking so much.

3 Rub the marmalade through a coarse sieve (strainer) to remove the rind, then rub a small amount into each breast. Reserve the remainder.

4 Heat a heavy-based frying pan (skillet) and fry (sauté) the duck breasts for about 5 minutes until the skin is brown and crisp. Transfer to an ovenproof dish and place in the oven for about 15 minutes until the meat is cooked to your liking; I like to leave duck slightly pink inside.

5 Heat the orange juice, port and reserved marmalade in a small saucepan and season with salt and pepper. Stir in the chicken stock, bring the sauce to a boil, then simmer until the quantity has reduced by half. Strain twice and keep the sauce warm.

6 Put the rice, water and olive oil in a large saucepan and bring to the boil. Cover and simmer for about 8 minutes until the rice is just tender. Drain.

7 Remove the duck from the oven and leave it to rest for 5 minutes before slicing.

8 Spoon the rice on to warm plates. Arrange the duck slices, fanned out with some of the sauce poured over.

Serving suggestions The ideal accompaniments are mashed potatoes and parsnips with some steamed greens, which give you great flavour, colour and texture.

vegetarian main courses

More and more people are eating vegetarian meals and this is just as true on board our yachts, so I am constantly looking for new meat-free recipes. There is no fish or meat in this section, but many recipes do use dairy products, so will not be suitable for vegans or strict vegetarians. Many Mediterranean recipes include wonderful fresh herbs such as parsley, basil, mint and rosemary, to name just a few. Adding just a handful of these to any dish can make all the difference. I love tomatoes, too, and so use them in lots of meals either as a base or to create a delicious and colourful sauce.

Cherry tomato pasta

I love to serve this wonderful bright, colourful dish just as it is, in plain white pasta bowls. You don't need to be a vegetarian to enjoy the flavour, especially liberally sprinkled with Parmesan.

SERVES 6–8

90 ml/6 tbsp olive oil

4 garlic cloves, crushed

Salt and freshly ground black pepper

1.5 kg/3 lb cherry tomatoes

2 small dried red chillies

250 ml/8 fl oz/1 cup water

50 g/2 oz/1 cup torn fresh basil leaves

1.25 kg/2½ lb farfalle or penne

1 bunch of fresh rocket leaves

50 g/2 oz/½ cup freshly shaved Parmesan cheese

1 Heat half the oil in a large frying pan (skillet) and fry (sauté) the garlic for a few minutes with lots of salt and pepper. Add the tomatoes and chillies and simmer gently for 5 minutes, stirring occasionally so that nothing sticks to the pan.

2 Add the water and continue to simmer for about 15 minutes until you have a thick sauce. Taste and adjust the seasoning. Discard the chillies, then stir in half the basil.

3 Bring a large pan of salted water to the boil, add the pasta and cook for about 8 minutes until just tender, then drain well.

4 Stir in the remaining olive oil, then add the tomato sauce and mix the sauce and pasta together well. Stir in the remaining basil.

5 Spoon the pasta into warm bowls and scatter generously with the rocket and Parmesan.

Serving suggestions Serve with a mixed salad and crusty bread.

Hints and variations I use this tomato sauce regularly with different pasta dishes such as lasagne, or as a sauce for sautéed veal or fish. If you cannot get cherry tomatoes, the best way to prepare this is to roast Roma or plum tomatoes in the oven for 1 hour with garlic and herbs and some olive oil, then crush these down to make a sauce.

Mediterranean flavour The cherry tomatoes you buy in Italy are hard to beat. They are stacked in piles on the market stalls still on their vines – baby and larger ones, round and oval – all so sweet as they have been sun-ripened in the strong Mediterranean sun. In the eastern Mediterranean, they even have a tomato festival in a place called Letoon in Turkey.

Frittata of artichoke hearts with roasted peppers

An Italian version of the Spanish omelette, this is generally baked rather than cooked on the hob. It always contains a variety of vegetables so is more colourful to look at than the plain Spanish omelette.

SERVES 6–8

10 eggs, beaten

120 ml/4 fl oz/½ cup milk

50 g/2 oz/½ cup freshly grated Parmesan cheese

Salt and freshly ground black pepper

15 ml/1 tbsp olive oil

400 g/14 oz/1 large jar of marinated artichoke hearts, drained and quartered

2 red (bell) peppers, roasted and sliced

25 g/1 oz/½ cup chopped fresh parsley

1 Preheat the oven to 180°C/350°F/gas 4/fan oven 160°C.

2 Beat the eggs with the milk and Parmesan. Season well with salt and pepper.

3 Heat the oil in a large ovenproof frying pan (skillet) and fry (sauté) the artichoke hearts and peppers for a few minutes, then add the parsley.

4 Pour the egg mixture over and stir together gently.

5 Place in the oven for 40–45 minutes until the frittata is well risen and golden brown.

6 Serve sliced into portions, with lots of parsley scattered over the top.

Serving suggestions This is wonderfully filling and needs nothing more than a crisp green salad.

Gorgonzola and pear quiche

Take a little time to arrange the pear slices in a 'fan' shape, so that you can see the fan once the quiche has been cooked. The flavour combination is delicious and it makes a really attractive lunch or supper dish.

SERVES 6–8

FOR THE SHORTCRUST PASTRY (BASIC PIE CRUST)
275 g/10 oz/2½ cups plain (all-purpose) flour

225 g/8 oz/1 cup butter, diced

1 egg, beaten

FOR THE FILLING
100 g/4 oz/1 cup Gorgonzola or blue cheese, crumbled

250 ml/8 fl oz/1 cup single (light) cream

3 eggs, beaten

Salt and freshly ground black pepper

4 pears, peeled, cored and thinly sliced

1 To make the pastry, sift the flour into a bowl and add the diced butter. Chop with a knife to blend into the flour and then gently use your fingertips to work the butter into the flour until it is the consistency of fine breadcrumbs. Do not overwork the dough but lift the mixture well, to aerate and keep it light.

2 Gradually add enough of the egg to form a dough. Knead lightly on a floured surface until smooth, then cover with clingfilm (plastic wrap) and chill in the fridge for at least 30 minutes.

3 Roll out the pastry on a lightly floured surface and use to line a 23 cm/9 in flan tin (pie pan). Prick all over the base with a fork and chill for a further 30 minutes.

4 Preheat the oven to 180°C/350°F/gas 4/fan oven 160°C.

5 Cover the pastry case (pie shell) with greaseproof (waxed) paper and fill with baking beans. Bake blind in the oven for 12 minutes. Remove the beans and paper, then return to the oven for 4 minutes. Remove from the oven and set aside.

6 To make the filling, melt the cheese in a saucepan over a very low heat with a small amount of the cream. Allow to cool, then stir in the rest of the cream and the eggs and season with salt and pepper.

7 Arrange the pear slices in a single layer in a fan pattern in the pastry case. Pour over some of the gorgonzola mixture, then continue to layer pear slices and cheese, finishing with a layer of cheese.

8 Bake in the oven for 30–40 minutes until well risen and golden. Allow to cool slightly before serving.

Serving suggestions My favourite accompaniment for this dish is a tomato, onion and caper salad.

Roasted tomato risotto

I was taught how to make a traditional risotto by an Italian guest. She never used scales. Since then I always measure my rice the way she taught me: two small handfuls per person. However, I've added measurements here.

SERVES 6–8

16 Roma tomatoes, halved lengthways

Salt and freshly ground black pepper

4 garlic cloves, crushed

60 ml/4 tbsp olive oil

2 onions, finely chopped

700 g/1½ lb/3 cups risotto (arborio) rice

4 sprigs of fresh thyme

1 sprig of fresh rosemary

750 ml/1¼ pts/3 cups hot water or stock

8 whole sun-dried tomatoes, roughly sliced

120 ml/4 fl oz/1 cup dry white wine

120–250 ml/4–8 fl oz/½–1 cup single (light) cream (optional)

25 g/1 oz/1 cup chopped fresh basil

25 g/1 oz/¼ cup freshly shaved Parmesan cheese

1 Preheat the oven to 180°C/350°F/gas 4/fan oven 160°C.

2 Arrange the tomatoes in a large baking dish. Season with salt and pepper, sprinkle with half the crushed garlic and drizzle with a little of the olive oil. Cook in the oven for 1 hour, turning over half way through cooking, until the tomatoes are soft and have caramelised.

3 Blend half the tomatoes to a purée and set them aside. Heat the remaining olive oil in a frying pan (skillet) and fry (sauté) the onions and the remaining garlic for about 5 minutes until soft. Add the rice, thyme and rosemary and stir to coat the rice with the oil.

4 Gradually add the hot water or stock a little at a time. Cook, stirring all the time, so that the rice absorbs the liquid before adding any more.

5 When you have added half the water or stock, stir in the sun-dried tomatoes and seasoning to taste, then continue adding the water or stock.

6 When you have added about three-quarters of the hot liquid, add the puréed tomatoes and wine, then continue with the liquid until the rice is tender but still has a slight bite and the risotto is creamy and moist.

7 Remove the thyme and rosemary sprigs. Reserve a roasted tomato half for each serving and add the remainder to the risotto. Season again to taste. Stir in the cream, if using, and the basil, cover and leave to stand for 5 minutes.

8 Spoon into warm bowls, sprinkle with the Parmesan and top each with a roasted tomato to serve.

Serving suggestions Serve this wonderful risotto with a green salad.

Hints and variations Make sure you don't add the wine and tomato purée too early otherwise the acid will prevent the rice from absorbing enough liquid.

Grilled polenta with peppers, mushrooms and onions

Polenta is a staple Italian dish. It can be made quite firm, then sliced and grilled or shaped into gnocchi; or you can make it looser and mix it with cheeses to serve with a salad. Do use a well-flavoured stock. See photograph opposite page 96.

SERVES 6–8

120 ml/4 fl oz/½ cup olive oil

1 onion, finely chopped

2 garlic cloves, chopped

225 g/8 oz mushrooms, finely chopped

75 g/3 oz/1½ cups chopped fresh parsley

1.2 litres/2 pts/5 cups vegetable stock

450 g/1 lb polenta

6 (bell) peppers

450 g/1 lb large whole mushrooms

6 red onions

120 ml/4 fl oz/½ cup white wine

Salt and freshly ground black pepper

1 Heat 30 ml/2 tbsp of the oil in a large saucepan and fry (sauté) the chopped onion, garlic and chopped mushrooms for about 5 minutes until soft. Stir in 25 g/1 oz/½ cup of the parsley, then add 450 ml/¾ pt/2 cups of the stock and bring to the boil.

2 Trickle in the polenta, stirring all the time and making sure no lumps form. Reduce the heat and cook very gently for about 20–30 minutes, stirring regularly to make sure the polenta does not stick. Once cooked, the polenta will be thick and come away easily from the side of the saucepan.

3 Pour the polenta into an oiled Swiss roll tin (jelly roll pan), level the surface and leave to cool, then chill for a couple of hours.

4 Preheat the oven to 200°C/400°F/gas 6/fan oven 180°C. Place the peppers, whole mushrooms and red onions in a baking tin (pan) and drizzle with half the remaining olive oil. Roast in the oven for about 30 minutes until cooked and browned.

5 Remove from the oven and place the peppers in a plastic bag for 15 minutes to cool and loosen the skins, then remove the skins and pull out the stalk and seeds. Slice the red onions and mushrooms.

6 Cut the polenta into small triangles and brush with the remaining oil. Grill (broil) for about 5 minutes on each side until golden brown.

7 Place the roasted vegetables in a saucepan with the remaining parsley, the wine and the remaining stock and heat through, stirring occasionally. Season to taste with salt and pepper. Serve the polenta slices with the hot vegetables on the side.

Serving suggestions A crispy Italian bread tastes good with this dish and will be useful to mop up the juices! If you don't have such a large appetite, go for a fresh salad.

Parmigiana di melanzane al siciliano

There are so many wonderful ways of cooking this dish. This version, which contains eggs, sets fairly firm and so is excellent for cutting into wedges as a lunch dish. Adding caster sugar to the sauce really brings out the sweetness of the tomatoes.

SERVES 6

3 large aubergines (eggplants)

60 ml/4 tbsp olive oil

4 garlic cloves, crushed

2 x 400 ml/14 fl oz/large cans of tomatoes, crushed

30 ml/2 tbsp tomato purée (paste)

5 ml/1 tsp caster (superfine) sugar

100 g/4 oz/2 cups fresh basil leaves, torn

Salt and freshly ground black pepper

1 onion, finely chopped

100 g/4 oz/2 cups fresh breadcrumbs

50 g/2 oz/1 cup chopped fresh parsley

100 g/4 oz/1 cup freshly grated Parmesan cheese

6 eggs

15 ml/1 tbsp milk

1 Cut the aubergines into slices about 5 mm/¼ in thick. Brush the slices with a little of the olive oil and grill (broil) for about 8 minutes on each side until lightly browned.

2 Heat 30 ml/2 tbsp of the olive oil in a frying pan (skillet) and fry (sauté) the garlic for a few minutes until soft. Add the tomatoes and cook for 10 minutes. Add the tomato purée and sugar and cook for a further 20 minutes until the sauce has thickened. Stir in the basil leaves at the last minute, then season to taste with salt and pepper.

3 Meanwhile, heat the remaining olive oil and fry the onion for a few minutes until opaque. Stir in the breadcrumbs. Remove from the heat, stir in the parsley and season well with salt and pepper.

4 Preheat the oven to 190°C/375°F/gas 5/fan oven 170°C.

5 Grease a rectangular ovenproof dish and sprinkle a third of the breadcrumb mixture over the bottom of the dish. Arrange half of the aubergine slices in a layer on top, then spoon over half the tomato sauce. Add another layer of breadcrumbs, then the remaining aubergines and tomato sauce. Finally add the remaining breadcrumbs and top with half the Parmesan cheese.

6 Beat together the eggs and milk, then pour over the dish, using a fork to pull the mixture from the side of the dish so that the liquid gets to the bottom and through the layers. Sprinkle with the remaining Parmesan and cook in the oven for 35–40 minutes until golden brown.

7 Serve on warm plates.

Serving suggestions I like to serve this with a hot tomato coulis sprinkled with fresh basil, and a tossed salad on the side.

Polenta pancakes and roasted vegetables

This is a useful alternative way to use polenta. It's a wonderfully colourful dish with the bright colours so typical of Mediterranean cuisine. I like my salsa hot – you may prefer to use fewer chillies!

SERVES 6–8

9 eggs

750 ml/1¼ pts/3 cups milk

275 g/10 oz/2½ cups plain (all-purpose) flour

50 g/2 oz/½ cup polenta

10 ml/2 tsp cayenne

4 red (bell) peppers

4 yellow peppers

4 courgettes (zucchini)

3 bulbs of fennel

60 ml/4 tbsp olive oil

1 bunch of fresh parsley, roughly chopped

Salt and freshly ground black pepper

500 ml/17 fl oz/2¼ cups plain yoghurt

1 Whisk together the eggs, milk, flour, polenta and cayenne until smooth, then leave to stand for 1 hour, stirring regularly.

2 Preheat the oven to 200°C/400°F/gas 6/fan oven 180°C.

3 Place the whole peppers, courgettes and fennel in a baking tin (pan) and drizzle with half the olive oil. Roast in the oven for about 30 minutes until browned.

4 Remove from the oven and place the peppers in a plastic bag for 15 minutes to cool, then remove the loosened skins and take the flesh off the stalk and seeds. Cut the flesh into strips. Thinly slice the fennel and slice the courgettes. Mix all the vegetables with the parsley and season with salt and pepper.

5 To make the corn salsa, chop half the corn finely and place it in a bowl. Add the remaining corn, then mix in the chillies, coriander, spring onions, tomatoes, cucumber and lemon juice and season well.

6 To cook the pancakes, heat the remaining oil in a frying pan (skillet) and spoon in a ladleful of the pancake mix, spreading it across the pan. Cook gently for a few minutes until firm, then turn and cook the other side. Turn out on to a plate and repeat with the rest of the mixture until you have about 12 pancakes.

7 While you are making the pancakes, gently warm the vegetable filling in a saucepan.

FOR THE SALSA

200 g/7 oz/1 small can of sweetcorn
(corn), drained

3 chillies, seeded and finely chopped

50 g/2 oz/1 cup chopped fresh
coriander (cilantro)

6 spring onions (scallions), chopped

2 tomatoes, chopped

½ cucumber, chopped

120 ml/4 fl oz/½ cup lemon juice

8 Lay a pancake on the work surface and spread with a layer of yoghurt, then place some vegetables on top. Roll the pancake up like a wrap, then cut in half. Repeat with the rest of the pancakes.

9 Serve the pancake pieces on warm plates with a spoonful of the corn salsa on the side.

Serving suggestions Just a tomato or pepper salad is all you need to make a complete meal of this dish.

Hints and variations You do need to leave the mixture to stand before cooking otherwise the polenta will not soften.

Grilled vegetable lasagne with fresh basil

If you have individual ovenproof dishes, you could make a lasagne for each of your guests. If you make them in advance, they will also heat through more quickly than one large one.

SERVES 6–8

4 red (bell) peppers

3 onions, roughly sliced

60 ml/4 tbsp olive oil

3 aubergines (eggplants), cut into 5 mm/¼ in thick slices

6 courgettes (zucchini), cut lengthways into 5 mm/¼ in thick slices

450 g/1 lb mushrooms

1 litre/1¾ pts/4¼ cups béchamel or white sauce

9 no-need-to-precook lasagne sheets

1 large bunch of fresh basil, torn

450 g/1 lb/4 cups grated Mozzarella cheese

50 g/2 oz/½ cup freshly grated Parmesan cheese

500 ml/17 fl oz/2¼ cups tomato sauce

Fresh basil leaves, to garnish

1 Preheat the oven 200°C/400°F/gas 6/fan oven 180°C.

2 Rub the peppers and onions with a little of the oil, then roast in the oven for about 30 minutes until browned.

3 Remove from the oven and place the peppers in a plastic bag for 15 minutes to cool and loosen the skins, then remove the skins and take the flesh off the stalk and seeds.

4 Brush the aubergine and courgette slices and the mushrooms with a little of the oil, then grill (broil) for about 8 minutes on each side until lightly browned.

5 Spoon a layer of béchamel sauce into an rectangular ovenproof dish. Place a layer of pasta sheets on top, then a layer of the grilled and roasted vegetables. Sprinkle some basil and Mozzarella on top. Continue layering the ingredients, finishing with a layer of pasta covered with béchamel sauce. Sprinkle with the Parmesan.

6 Cook in the oven for about 30 minutes until golden and bubbling hot.

7 Heat through the tomato sauce.

8 Cut the lasagne into portions and place on warm plates. Serve with some tomato sauce and scatter a few fresh basil leaves over to garnish.

Serving suggestions This is best accompanied with a mixed green salad.

Hints and variations If you prefer not to oil the vegetables, simply grill them without oil.

Pasta puttanesca

This is a classic Italian pasta dish with a spicy tomato sauce that takes full advantage of some the Mediterranean's finest ingredients: olives, capers and basil. Use whichever pasta shape you prefer. I use penne as it holds the sauce inside the tubes.

SERVES 6–8

120 ml/4 fl oz/½ cup olive oil

6 garlic cloves, crushed

2 x 400 ml/14 fl oz/large cans of tomatoes

4 whole red chillies

175 g/6 oz/1 cup stoned (pitted) black olives

50 g/2 oz/½ cup capers, rinsed and drained

Salt and freshly ground black pepper

700–900 g/1½–2 lb penne

50 g/2 oz/1 cup torn fresh basil leaves

A few sprigs of fresh basil

50 g/2 oz/½ cup freshly shaved Parmesan cheese

1 Heat 30 ml/2 tbsp of the olive oil in a saucepan and fry (sauté) the garlic for a few minutes until soft. Stir in the tomatoes and chillies and simmer for 15 minutes.

2 Add the olives and capers and continue to cook for a further 15 minutes, stirring regularly. Season to taste with salt and pepper.

3 Bring a large pan of salted water to the boil, add the pasta and boil for about 10 minutes until al dente. Drain and toss with the remaining olive oil.

4 Toss the basil leaves into the tomato sauce. Remove the whole chillies and pour the sauce over the pasta.

5 Serve in individual pasta bowls with a sprig of basil and some shaved Parmesan on top.

Serving suggestion I always offer a green salad on the side.

Hints and variations If you eat fish you can add 50 g/2 oz/1 small can of anchovies, drained, with the garlic and oil.

Mediterranean flavour Gaeta is the most famous area for olives in Italy. The old town with its colourful buildings is situated high on the hill, while the new town is set further down next to the sparkling waters of the bay.

Roasted tomato pasta with peppers, garlic and basil

I often use pasta in my cooking. Add those other favourites – sun-ripened tomatoes and basil – and you have the basis of a delicious lunch or supper dish. I make lots of this sauce with and without peppers and freeze it so that we can still enjoy it during the winter.

SERVES 6–8

1 kg/2¼ lb Roma tomatoes

1 garlic clove, crushed

Salt and freshly ground black pepper

250 ml/8 fl oz/1 cup olive oil

4 red or yellow (bell) peppers

700–900 g/1½–2 lb linguine

1 bunch of fresh basil, roughly torn

100 g/4 oz/1 cup freshly grated Parmesan cheese

1 Preheat the oven to 200°C/400°F/gas 6/fan oven 180°C.

2 Slice the tomatoes in half, place in a baking tin (pan) and sprinkle with the garlic. Season well with salt and pepper, then drizzle with a little of the olive oil. Roast in the oven for at least 1 hour until soft.

3 Meanwhile, rub the peppers with a little oil, place on a baking (cookie) sheet and roast in the oven for about 30 minutes. Remove from the oven and place in a plastic bag for 15 minutes, then remove the loosened skins and discard the stalk and seeds.

4 Place the tomatoes and peppers in a blender and pulse until coarsely blended. Place in a saucepan, season with salt and pepper and keep warm as you cook the pasta.

5 Bring a large pan of salted water to the boil, add the linguine and boil for about 10 minutes until al dente, then drain.

6 Toss the basil into the tomato sauce, then pour over the pasta and serve sprinkled with the Parmesan.

Serving suggestions One of my favourite accompaniments to this dish is a tossed green salad of mixed leaves and herbs such as parsley, basil and chives.

Roasted peppers stuffed with tomatoes and parmesan

These look great on any table setting, bringing the taste and colours of summer even in the midst of winter. All the flavours are traditionally Mediterranean and the recipe is simplicity itself to prepare. Obviously the anchovies are optional.

SERVES 6

3 large red (bell) peppers

2 garlic cloves, finely chopped

6 cherry tomatoes, halved

Salt and freshly ground black pepper

30 ml/2 tbsp olive oil

6 anchovy fillets, halved (optional)

25 g/1 oz/½ cup chopped fresh basil leaves

100 g/4 oz/1 cup freshly shaved Parmesan cheese

1 Preheat the oven 180°C/350°F/gas 4/fan oven 160°C.

2 Cut the peppers in half lengthways and carefully remove the cores without cutting off the stalk area. Take out all the seeds.

3 Lay all the halves rounded-side down on a baking (cookie) sheet and sprinkle the insides with half the garlic. Put two of the cherry tomato halves in each pepper, then add the remaining garlic and season well with salt and pepper. Sprinkle with the olive oil.

4 Roast in the oven for 30 minutes. Add an anchovy fillet, if using, to each pepper half, sprinkle with half the basil and roast for a further 5 minutes.

5 Serve on individual plates, garnished with the remaining basil and the Parmesan.

Serving suggestions You can serve these on their own as a starter or side dish, or with rice as a main course.

Roasted camembert parcels with mixed salad

These delightful golden brown parcels look great on a bed of mixed salad leaves. If you wish, you can cut them open so that the cooked, melted cheese oozes out on to the plate – delicious!

SERVES 6

**3 large sheets of filo pastry (paste),
each cut into six 5 cm/2 in squares**

Olive oil, for brushing

3 whole Camembert cheeses

**25 g/1 oz/½ cup chopped mixed
fresh herbs**

2 garlic cloves, crushed

1 small red chilli, finely chopped

15 ml/1 tbsp sesame seeds

100 g/4 oz baby spinach leaves

100 g/4 oz baby rocket leaves

100 g/4 oz mizuna leaves

100 g/4 oz cherry tomatoes

1 large red onion, thinly sliced

15 ml/1 tbsp sunflower seeds

FOR THE VINAIGRETTE

45 ml/3 tbsp balsamic vinegar

5 ml/1 tsp wholegrain mustard

15 ml/1 tbsp clear honey

1 Preheat the oven to 180°C/350°F/gas 4/fan oven 160°C.

2 Brush the squares of filo with olive oil, then place two pieces one on top of the other. Repeat with all the pastry. As filo pastry is so fine and dries out very quickly, make sure you cover the pastry you are not using with clingfilm (plastic wrap) and then a damp tea towel (dish cloth).

3 Cut each cheese into six rounds using a 3 cm/1¼ in round biscuit (cookie) cutter, then slice each in half horizontally.

4 Mix together the herbs, garlic and chilli.

5 Place half the Camembert slices on stacks of filo, add some of the herb and garlic mixture, then top with the remaining Camembert. Brush the edges of the filo with a little more oil. Bring the filo up and over the Camembert and twist it together at the top. Arrange on a greased baking (cookie) sheet and sprinkle with sesame seeds.

6 Bake in the oven for 35 minutes until golden.

7 Mix together the salad leaves, tomatoes, onion and sunflower seeds and arrange on individual plates.

8 Whisk together the vinaigrette ingredients and pour over the salad. Top with the baked Camembert parcels and serve at once.

Hints and variations You can prepare the parcels in advance and then cover them with clingfilm (plastic wrap) and keep them, uncooked, in the fridge for a few hours, ready for baking when you are ready.

salads and side dishes

This is a versatile collection of recipes: most of them can be used as side dishes, starters or light lunches, on their own or with a serving of crusty bread. It is fun making a variety of salads with the different salad leaves that are available, and the markets in the South of France and Italy often sell mixed salad leaves, washed and trimmed, ready to dress. They sell baby rocket and spinach leaves this way, too, whereas in Spain, Greece and Croatia you can only buy certain salad heads. Most people buy their prepared salad leaves in small bags, so the stallholders are often quite taken aback when I ask for a kilo!

Watermelon salad with feta, kiwi and red onion

*The colour of watermelon is so vibrant in the middle of summer and the flesh makes
a pleasant change in this salad, which is particularly refreshing in the very hot months.
Toasted pumpkin seeds add a delicious crunch.*

SERVES 6–8

FOR THE SALAD
150 g/5 oz/1¼ cups pumpkin seeds

½ large watermelon, peeled and diced
into 1 cm/½ in chunks

300 g/11 oz/1¼ cups Feta cheese,
diced

2 red onions, sliced

25 g/1 oz/½ cup roughly chopped
fresh mint

1 kiwi fruit, peeled and very thinly
sliced lengthways

Salt and freshly ground black pepper

FOR THE CITRUS DRESSING
60 ml/4 tbsp olive oil

30 ml/2 tbsp lemon juice

5 ml/1 tsp Dijon mustard

5 ml/1 tsp clear honey

1 Toast the pumpkin seeds in a dry saucepan for a few minutes until aromatic, shaking the pan and removing them from the pan as soon as they are browned so that they do not burn. Set aside to cool.

2 Mix all the salad ingredients in a bowl and season with salt and pepper.

3 Mix all the ingredients for the dressing together with plenty of salt and pepper.

4 Serve the salad on individual plates with the dressing on the side and the toasted pumpkin seeds sprinkled on top.

Hints and variations The Citrus Dressing is very versatile – I sometimes add a dash of Tabasco or soy sauce, depending on what I am using it for, but with the watermelon it is best left just as it is. You can also substitute lime or orange juice for the lemon juice when you are using this dressing for other salads.

Mediterranean flavour You see watermelon sellers by the side of the road, their trucks loaded with melons, in all the southern Mediterranean countries. Some of the fruit are so heavy and large that I simply wouldn't have space for them in my limited onboard storage.

In Greece, fresh watermelon juice was the soft drink all the children wanted during the long, hot summer months before the introduction of American fizzy drinks.

Caesar salad with blackened prawns

The traditional Caesar salad is delicious for any occasion but it is fun to jazz it up with other meats or fish with the bacon. The quantity of spice mix is plenty for several dishes and you can store it in an airtight container. See photograph opposite page 97.

SERVES 6–8

FOR THE BLACKENED SPICE MIX
15 ml/1 tbsp sweet paprika

12.5 ml/2½ tsp salt

5 ml/1 tsp each onion powder, garlic powder and cayenne

4 ml/¾ tsp each ground white pepper and coarsely ground black pepper

2.5 ml/½ tsp each dried thyme and dried oregano

FOR THE SALAD
300 g/11 oz pieces of pancetta or bacon

120 ml/4 fl oz/½ cup plain yoghurt

120 ml/4 fl oz/½ cup olive oil

64 large raw king prawns (jumbo shrimp), peeled and deveined

100 g/4 oz/1 cup croûtons

2 large cos lettuces, torn into pieces

150 g/5 oz/1¼ cups freshly grated Parmesan cheese

50 g/2 oz/1 small can of anchovies, drained and crushed

250 ml/8 fl oz/1 cup Home-made Mayonnaise (see page 29)

Salt and freshly ground black pepper

50 g/2 oz/½ cup freshly shaved Parmesan cheese

1 Preheat the oven to 180°C/350°F/gas 4/fan oven 160°C.

2 Mix together the spices and herbs for the blackened spice mix.

3 Place the pancetta or bacon pieces in a roasting tin (pan) and cook in the oven for about 10 minutes until cooked, watching them carefully as they burn easily. Remove from the oven and place on two layers of kitchen paper (paper towel) to drain off the fat and allow to cool.

4 Place the yoghurt in a sieve (strainer) lined with muslin (cheesecloth) and leave to drain.

5 Pour the olive oil into a bowl or plate and add 15 ml/1 tbsp of the blackened spice mix. Mix these two together well. Roll the prawns in the mixture.

6 Heat a large heavy-based frying pan (skillet) and fry (sauté) the prawns over a high heat for a few minutes, tossing them until they turn pink.

7 Mix the pancetta or bacon pieces with the croûtons, the lettuce and half the grated Parmesan.

8 Mix the anchovies into the mayonnaise, then blend with the drained yoghurt and season with salt and pepper. Stir in the remaining grated Parmesan. Pour over the salad and toss well.

9 Arrange the salad on a large platter with the prawns scattered around the edge. Sprinkle generously with the shaved Parmesan before serving.

Hints and variations This could also be a starter or light lunch, or a rich side salad if the blackened prawns are omitted.

Goats' cheese salad with tapenade

*This colourful and tasty salad is very popular in France. I love the flavour of goats'
cheese and it is now readily available in supermarkets and the local markets where I
shop. This is a great way of using up leftover baguette as it doesn't have to be fresh.*

SERVES 6–8

**30 ml/2 tbsp crushed pink
peppercorns**

**15 ml/1 tbsp crushed black
peppercorns**

15 ml/1 tbsp salt

45 ml/3 tbsp lemon juice

120 ml/4 fl oz/½ cup olive oil

**350 g/12 oz goats' cheese with a rind,
cut into 5 mm/¼ in slices**

1 baguette

30 ml/2 tbsp tapenade

30 ml/2 tbsp sun-dried tomato pesto

400 g/14 oz mixed salad leaves

24 cherry tomatoes, halved

1 Mix the pink and black peppercorns and the salt with the lemon
juice and 45 ml/3 tbsp of the olive oil in a shallow bowl. Add the
cheese slices and leave to marinate for 1 hour.

2 Preheat the oven to 180°C/350°F/gas 4/fan oven 160°C.

3 Cut the baguette thinly into at least 24 slices. Brush one side of each
slice with the remaining olive oil and arrange in a baking tin (pan).

4 Spread a little tapenade on the unoiled sides of half the bread slices.
Spread the remaining slices with the sun-dried tomato pesto, also
on the unoiled sides. Lift the cheese from the marinade and place on
top. Drizzle with the peppered olive oil and bake in the oven for
10–15 minutes until the cheese is golden brown.

5 Arrange the salad leaves and cherry tomatoes on individual plates.
Top with the baked goats' cheese slices and serve.

Hints and variations Crumble some pan-fried proscuitto into the
salad to add a salty flavour and balance the flavour of the goats'
cheese.

Fresh borlotti bean salad with olives

Borlotti beans are popular in the Mediterranean and can be bought from June to late September. The green and white pods are speckled with pinky-purple and the beans inside are also speckled, but this colour is lost once they are cooked.

SERVES 6–8

1 kg/2¼ lb borlotti beans, removed from the pods

150 ml/¼ pt/⅔ cup olive oil

Juice of 2 lemons

2 garlic cloves, crushed

Salt and freshly ground black pepper

1 red onion, finely chopped

6 sun-dried tomatoes, chopped

4 tomatoes, seeded and diced

75 g/3 oz/½ cup stoned (pitted) olives, finely chopped

1 bunch of spring onions (scallions), finely chopped

50 g/2 oz/1 cup chopped fresh parsley

1 Place the beans in a large pan of water, bring to the boil and boil for 25–30 minutes or until soft. Drain well, rinse under cold water and drain again.

2 Whisk together the olive oil, lemon juice and garlic and season well with salt and pepper.

3 Put the beans into a bowl, pour over the dressing and mix well. Taste and adjust the seasoning if necessary.

4 Add the remaining ingredients and toss well.

5 Set aside to chill for about 30 minutes before serving to allow the flavours to blend.

Serving suggestions I like to serve this on a bed of rocket with some lemon wedges on the side – the contrast of colours is wonderful.

Hints and variations If you cannot find borlotti beans, you can use broad (lima) beans. You can also use canned beans, if you are in a hurry.

You can halve the amount of parsley and add 150 g/5 oz of chopped rocket.

Quails' egg and walnut salad

*I like to use quails' eggs in this salad but hens' eggs are fine – use just one hen's egg
per person and quarter them. Quails' eggs only take 3–4 minutes to hard-boil.
A careful presentation makes a big difference to the effect.*

SERVES 6–8

300 g/11 oz baby spinach leaves

**2 heads of chicory (Belgian endive),
divided into leaves**

1 bunch of rocket

1 red onion, thinly sliced

**100 g/4 oz/1 cup walnuts, roughly
chopped**

**18 quails' eggs, hard-boiled (hard-
cooked) and peeled**

120 ml/4 fl oz/½ cup olive oil

10 ml/2 tsp lemon juice

15 ml/1 tbsp wholegrain mustard

Salt and freshly ground black pepper

1 Toss together the spinach leaves, chicory, rocket, onion and walnuts
and arrange on a large platter.

2 Peel 12 of the eggs, slice in half and arrange on the salad.

3 Whisk together the olive oil, lemon juice and mustard and season
well with salt and pepper. Pour over the salad.

4 Peel half of the shell of each of the last six eggs, leaving the other
half on for decoration.

5 Arrange on the salad and serve.

Hints and variations If you are using hen's eggs instead of quails',
you can make a slightly different salad. Poach the eggs for
8 minutes and serve them warm on top of the salad with the
dressing drizzled over.

Photograph opposite:
**Grilled Polenta with Peppers, Mushrooms
and Onions (see page 82)**

Pickled spicy bean salad

A side dish with a little kick, you can serve this straight from the saucepan but it works equally well if the beans have cooled. They look great on a large white platter, which contrasts perfectly with the green and red of the chilli.

SERVES 6–8

600 ml/1 pt/2½ cups white wine vinegar

4 small dried red chillies

15 ml/1 tbsp black peppercorns

30 ml/2 tbsp dried coriander (cilantro) seeds

5 ml/1 tsp salt

900 g/2 lb French (green) beans, topped and tailed

120 ml/4 fl oz/½ cup olive oil

1 Pour about 750 ml/1¼ pts/3 cups water into a large saucepan and add the vinegar, chillies, peppercorns, coriander seeds and salt. Bring slowly to the boil.

2 Add the beans and return to the boil, then reduce the heat and simmer for 20 minutes. (The large quantity of vinegar in the saucepan means that the beans are almost being pickled.)

3 Drain well, discarding all the spices. Arrange on a serving dish, pour over the olive oil and chill until ready to serve.

Serving suggestion This recipe makes a wonderful addition to an antipasta platter.

Photograph opposite:
**Caesar Salad with Blackened Prawns
(see page 93)**

Greek salad

You couldn't publish a book of this kind without including a great Greek salad. The traditional salad is an art in itself as the Greeks will only eat it if the tomatoes and cucumber have been cut a certain way! Plus the Feta has to be of the highest quality.

SERVES 6–8

1 large cucumber

2 bunches of rocket

12 tomatoes, roughly chopped

½ green (bell) pepper, sliced into rings

½ red or orange pepper, sliced into rings

1 large red onion, sliced

175 g/6 oz/1 cup stoned (pitted) black olives

250 g/9 oz/generous 2 cups Feta cheese, diced

5 ml/1 tsp dried oregano

120 ml/4 fl oz/½ cup olive oil

Salt and freshly ground black pepper

1 Peel the cucumber lengthways, leaving three strips of skin on to give a striped appearance. Slice in half lengthways, then thickly slice the halves.

2 Divide the rocket between the plates, then arrange the rest of the vegetables over the top.

3 Sprinkle with the olives, then the Feta cheese and oregano. Drizzle with the olive oil, season with salt and pepper and serve.

Serving suggestion I like to scatter a few caper leaf stalks and seed heads over the top for a really authentic Greek touch.

Mediterranean flavour The Greek islands are very special, each different in its own way. Sailing around them is a great experience as you can find some wonderful restaurants with real traditional foods. I was lucky enough to be taught many of my Greek dishes by some very close friends who own a fish taverna in Rhodes. They produce the best of the best traditional food, which makes their restaurant a huge success, of course.

Tomato and mozzarella salad

An Italian salad or starter dish, this is called insalata caprese *and is sometimes served with prosciutto. You can present this either on one large platter or on individual plates, whichever you prefer.*

SERVES 6–8

6 large sun-ripened tomatoes, sliced

400 g/14 oz Mozzarella cheese, sliced

Salt and freshly ground black pepper

50 g/2 oz/1 cup small basil leaves

120 ml/4 fl oz/½ cup olive oil

175 g/6 oz/1 cup stoned (pitted) black olives

1 Arrange the tomatoes and Mozzarella alternately in patterns on individual plates and season generously with salt and pepper.

2 Tear up the basil leaves and sprinkle them over the tomato and Mozzarella, then drizzle with the olive oil and scatter the olives on the top.

Serving suggestions This one really needs lots of crusty ciabatta bread to mop up the delicious juices. The Italians always provide extra olive oil and balsamic vinegar too.

Hints and variations Use the freshest, best-quality Mozzarella you can find. If possible, choose buffalo-milk Mozzarella, which really has a superb flavour.

Mediterranean flavour Mozzarella comes in several different sizes and shapes in the Italian markets, usually either rounds or fat plaits. It is very different to some of the processed Mozzarella we are used to from the supermarkets and is a must to try if you are in Italy.

In Italian restaurants, you order the Mozzarella by the weight of how much you want to eat and the tomatoes and basil come as a side salad.

Avocado salad with lime and chilli

This versatile side dish is really like a guacamole salad, which you can use to top crostini (see page 21), or as a salsa with grilled meats or fish. It has a wonderful contrast of flavours and textures.

SERVES 6

3 ripe avocados, peeled and stoned (pitted)

Juice of 2 lemons

4 large tomatoes, seeded and cut into 1 cm/¹⁄₂ in dice

1 red onion, chopped

1 red (bell) pepper, cut into 1 cm/¹⁄₂ in dice

¹⁄₂ fresh green chilli, seeded and finely chopped

Salt and freshly ground black pepper

1 bunch of fresh coriander (cilantro), chopped

A few slices of lime or lemon

1 Cut the avocado into 1 cm/¹⁄₂ in dice and toss immediately in half the lemon juice to prevent it from browning.

2 Mix with the tomatoes, onion, pepper and chilli and season well with salt and pepper.

3 Toss with the remaining lemon juice and the coriander.

4 Serve on individual plates garnished with lemon or lime slices.

Hints and variations Dice the vegetables into fairly large pieces so that they do not collapse when you toss the salad. You can also omit the chilli if you prefer or add more, as I do – especially when I find fresh jalapeño chillies.

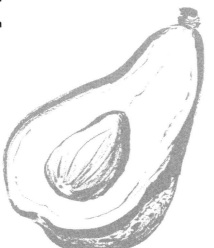

Walnut and orange salad with garlic croûtons

This salad takes only minutes to prepare and has a wonderful fresh taste. The crunchy walnuts, toasted in a dry pan, complement the oranges and the onion gives it a bit of bite.

SERVES 6–8

100 g/4 oz/1 cup walnuts, toasted and roughly chopped

2 oranges, peeled, segmented and chopped

1 white onion, thinly sliced

200 g/8 oz/2 cups garlic croûtons (see page 14)

400 g/14 oz baby spinach and rocket leaves

100 g/4 oz/1 cup freshly shaved Parmesan cheese

120 ml/4 fl oz/½ cup balsamic vinegar

120 ml/4 fl oz/½ cup olive oil

1 Toss together all the ingredients except the Parmesan, vinegar and olive oil.

2 Place the salad on individual plates and sprinkle with the Parmesan.

3 Mix together the balsamic vinegar and olive oil and place a spoonful on the side of each plate before serving.

Hints and variations You can use Feta cheese instead of Parmesan, if you like, crumbling it into the salad, or shaved Pecorino cheese.

Basmati rice with roasted spices and nuts

This rice adds a great flavour to a simple curry or you can team it with any other
Indian dishes. I also find it works well with plain grilled meats.

SERVES 6–8

15 ml/1 tbsp coriander (cilantro) seeds

15 ml/1 tbsp sesame seeds

15 ml/1 tbsp white mustard seeds

15 ml/1 tbsp cardamom pods

30 ml/2 tbsp olive oil

100 g/4 oz/1 cup cashew nuts,
roughly chopped

100 g/4 oz/1 cup almonds,
roughly chopped

1 cinnamon stick

5 ml/1 tsp salt

450 g/1 lb/2 cups basmati rice, washed

850 ml/1⅓ pts/3½ cups water

1 Toast the coriander, sesame, mustard and cardamom seeds in a dry pan for a few minutes until aromatic. Remove the cardamom seeds from the pods and then grind all the seeds.

2 Heat the oil in a large saucepan and add the ground spices, nuts, cinnamon, salt and rice. Stir well so the rice is coated in the flavoured oil.

3 Add the water and bring to the boil. Cover, reduce the heat and simmer for 20 minutes until all the water has been absorbed.

4 Discard the cinnamon stick and fluff up the rice with a fork before serving.

Serving suggestions I like to serve this rice on a large platter, with the top decorated with edible gold or silver leaves.

Hints and variations You could add the zest of 2 lemons and replace 120 ml/4 fl oz/½ cup of the water with the same measure of lemon juice. Adding slices of preserved lemon to the cooked rice gives a wonderful North African flavour.

Indian flavour! Basmati is an Indian rice, which comes in several different varieties. I was taught by an Indian chef from Kerala that you must wash the rice three times before you cook it: 'Once to clean it, twice to wash away the starch and three times for the fact that the rice loves us to eat it,' he told me.

Grilled field mushrooms with garlic and chilli

If you can find large field mushrooms, this is a great way to serve them as a starter or side dish, or as a lunch dish with just a fresh green salad. Smaller mushrooms can also be prepared in this way.

SERVES 6

**12 large field mushrooms,
about 7.5 cm/3 in in diameter**

45 ml/3 tbsp olive oil

Salt and freshly ground black pepper

3 garlic cloves, crushed

**1 green chilli, seeded and
finely chopped**

**50 g/2 oz/1 cup roughly chopped
fresh parsley**

1 Clean the mushrooms and remove the stalks, which you can reserve and use for stock. Toss the mushrooms in half the oil, season with salt and pepper and arrange in a shallow baking tin (pan).

2 Grill (broil) under a hot grill (broiler) for about 10 minutes until tender, turning once.

3 Meanwhile, heat the remaining oil in a frying pan (skillet) and fry (sauté) the garlic and chilli for a few minutes until soft, then stir in half the parsley.

4 Place the mushrooms on individual plates. Mix any cooking juices from the mushrooms into the frying pan, then pour the mixture over the mushrooms. Sprinkle with the remaining parsley before serving.

Hints and variations Portobello mushrooms work extremely well in this recipe.

Mediterranean flavour In San Remo in northern Italy, there is a wonderful family restaurant set beside a fast-flowing river where they specialise in mushrooms. For starters, there are often fresh porcini, ceps, chanterelles and other wild mushrooms that have been collected that day and cooked in a variety of ways. The main dish is often of lamb or beef with an accompaniment of breaded or sautéed mushrooms, served with the local red or white wine. Finally, for dessert, they offer a large bowl of tiramisu.

SALADS AND SIDE DISHES

Baby spinach salad with apples, mango and feta

I love the combination of colours, textures and flavours in this fresh dish. I find that fruit always adds an interesting dimension to salads and works well with all kinds of grilled or roasted meats.

SERVES 6–8

4 apples, peeled, cored and cut into 5 mm/¼ in slices

2 ripe mangos, peeled and stoned (pitted)

200 g/7 oz/generous ¾ cup Feta cheese, diced

300 g/11 oz baby spinach leaves

1 quantity of Citrus Dressing (see page 92)

Salt and freshly ground black pepper

1 Preheat the oven to 140°C/275°F/gas 1/fan oven 125°C.

2 Arrange the apple slices on a baking (cookie) sheet and dry out in the oven for about 3 hours. Alternatively, leave out in the sun for a few days. They should still be moist and pliable.

3 Slice the mangos and chop the flesh into fine matchsticks. Toss with the rest of the ingredients, then season with salt and pepper.

4 Serve the salad on individual plates.

Serving suggestions This is a dish that I enjoy serving as it is perfect as either a side salad with grilled (broiled) fish and chicken or as a main course on its own, in which case this quantity will serve 4 to 6 people.

Hints and variations You can change the apple and mango for cucumber and cantaloupe melon, which works just as well.

Roasted peppers with rocket, anchovy and parmesan

You can use any combination of colours of peppers you like or just one colour if you prefer, although I think the salad looks stunning using as many different colours as I can find.

SERVES 6–8

2 red (bell) peppers

2 yellow peppers

2 orange peppers

3 garlic cloves, chopped

60 ml/4 tbsp olive oil

300 g/11 oz rocket, roughly chopped

50 g/2 oz/1 small can of anchovies, drained, rinsed and sliced into strips

100 g/4 oz/1 cup freshly shaved Parmesan cheese

Freshly ground black pepper

1 Preheat the oven to 200°C/400°F/gas 6/fan oven 180°C.

2 Place the whole peppers in a baking tin (pan) and roast in the oven for about 30–40 minutes, turning once, until their skins are blistering and scorched. Remove from oven and place in a plastic bag to sweat for 15 minutes.

3 Rub to remove the skins. Discard the seeds, tear the flesh into strips and place in a bowl with the cooking juices. Add the garlic and olive oil and leave to marinate for 1 hour.

4 Arrange the rocket on individual plates and place the strips of pepper on top. Garnish with the anchovy strips, scatter with Parmesan shavings and drizzle over the garlic-flavoured olive oil. Season well with black pepper before serving.

Mediterranean flavour Travelling around Italian markets along the coastline, as I do, is a colourful affair with all the fresh fruit and vegetables on display. The Mediterranean sunlight seems to make everything much more vivid. The peppers are particularly wonderful there, as are the cherry tomatoes, fresh from the fields and still on their vines.

Grilled vegetables with a hot balsamic dressing

Grilled vegetables are popular as an antipasta dish in Italy, but I often serve them with the main course as they make a fun dish that complements lots of main courses and they are so easy to prepare.

SERVES 6–8

2 medium aubergines (eggplants)

4 courgettes (zucchini)

2 red or yellow (bell) peppers

30 ml/2 tbsp olive oil

2 garlic cloves, thinly sliced

90 ml/6 tbsp balsamic vinegar

10 fresh basil leaves, torn

Salt and freshly ground black pepper

TO SERVE
Shaved Parmesan cheese

6 fresh basil leaves, torn

1 Cut the aubergine into 5 mm/¼ in slices. Slice the courgette lengthways into slices no longer than 6 cm/2½ in. If the courgettes are long, cut them in half. Slice the peppers into long pieces from the core downwards so that you get flattish pieces rather than rounds.

2 Heat a grill (broiler) pan and grill the vegetables over a medium heat until they are charred and tender. Place on a platter while you make the dressing.

3 Heat the olive oil in a small saucepan and add the garlic and balsamic vinegar. Once the dressing has come to the boil, turn off the heat, add the basil leaves and season to taste. Pour over the grilled vegetables.

4 Serve hot or cold sprinkled with Parmesan and scattered with basil.

Mediterranean flavour Italian people are among the most demanding to cook for, as they are so traditional and love their own regional cooking. It's a good thing their produce is of such high quality, so that I can always give them the very best cuisine.

Spring onion and potato purée

These potatoes have a fresh flavour and make a delicious change from normal plain puréed potato or mashed potato. Use Maris Piper or King Edward for best results.

SERVES 6–8

6 large potatoes

Salt and freshly ground black pepper

15 g/½ oz/1 tbsp butter

250 ml/8 fl oz/1 cup milk

1 bunch of spring onions (scallions), thinly sliced

1 Place the potatoes in a saucepan, cover with water and add a pinch of salt. Bring to the boil, then reduce the heat and simmer for 30 minutes until soft enough to mash.

2 Drain the potatoes and mash well. Add the butter and enough of the milk to make the consistency you prefer.

3 Stir in the spring onions and season well with salt and pepper before serving.

Serving suggestions Serve with grilled (broiled) meat, chicken or fish, or with any main course you would accompany with mashed potatoes.

Hints and variations Slice both the white and green parts of the spring onions to add colour to the dish. If you have any leftovers, you can make tasty potato cakes for the next day.

You could also add 30 ml/2 tbsp of grated Parmesan cheese or a whole head of roasted garlic.

Potato and cashew nut curry with coconut milk

This is quite a rich dish, full of wonderful flavour. It can be used as a starter or a side dish to go with other curries. I like to serve a couple of different curry dishes with some plain rice and naan.

SERVES 6–8

900 g/2 lb potatoes, cut into 2 cm/¾ in dice

275 g/10 oz/2½ cups unsalted cashew nuts

15 ml/1 tbsp coriander (cilantro) seeds

45 ml/3 tbsp olive oil

15 ml/1 tbsp Madras curry powder

200 ml/7 fl oz/scant 1 cup single (light) cream

120 ml/4 fl oz/½ cup full-fat coconut milk

Salt and freshly ground black pepper

50 g/2 oz/1 cup roughly chopped fresh coriander

1 Place the potatoes in a saucepan of water and bring to the boil. Cook for 10–15 minutes until tender but not breaking up. Drain well.

2 Toss the cashew nuts in a dry frying pan (skillet) for a few minutes, watching them carefully so they do not burn.

3 Toast the coriander seeds in the same way, then grind them using a pestle and mortar.

4 Heat the olive oil in a large frying pan and gently fry (sauté) the potato pieces with the coriander seeds and curry powder, stirring to coat the potatoes in the spices.

5 Add the cashew nuts. Pour on the cream and coconut milk and heat through gently. Season with salt and pepper and add the chopped coriander at the last minute, just before serving.

Hints and variations You can make your own Madras-style curry powder with a mixture of ground cinnamon, bay leaves, cloves and cardamom seeds. Unsalted cashews are available in major supermarkets, delicatessens or ethnic stores. You can substitute almonds or unsalted peanuts, if you prefer.

Indian flavour Having visited a cashew nut factory in India, I now realise why they are so expensive – the amount of work involved in toasting them is unbelievable!

Banana raita with fresh coriander

This side dish offers a very unusual combination of flavours. The sweetness of the bananas is offset by the tang of garlic, with the selection of traditional spices adding a further dimension.

SERVES 6–8

25 g/1 oz/2 tbsp butter

1 onion

1 garlic clove, crushed

5 ml/1 tsp coriander (cilantro) seeds, crushed

2.5 ml/¹⁄₂ tsp cumin seeds, crushed

30 ml/2 tbsp ground turmeric

4–6 ripe bananas, sliced

300 ml/¹⁄₂ pt/1¹⁄₄ cups plain yoghurt

25 g/1 oz/¹⁄₂ cup chopped fresh coriander

1 Melt the butter in a frying pan (skillet) and fry (sauté) the onion and garlic until they are opaque.

2 Add the spices and stir in well. Add the bananas, stir to coat the pieces with the spices, then cook for a few minutes until they start to break down.

3 Reduce the heat to a minimum and gradually add the yoghurt, stirring continuously. If the heat is too high, the mixture will curdle.

4 Stir in the fresh coriander.

5 Serve warm, or cool and serve chilled.

Serving suggestions This is delicious as an accompaniment to curries or grilled (broiled) fish or meats.

Hints and variations If you want to make this really authentic, then use ghee instead of butter.

desserts

I love making desserts. Even in the heat of the Mediterranean, guests find it very hard to say no to a rich chocolate cake or a fresh fruit tart. Teatime treats are popular too. On some cruises, I bake cookies and cakes almost daily and serve them with cappuccino or afternoon tea or coffee.

You'll quickly notice that I pull in dessert ideas from all over the place – not just the Mediterranean – but I especially like to use fresh fruit from the local markets, so I always have lots available to make fabulous desserts, ice creams, sorbets and fruit coulis.

Italian lemon pudding with fresh berries

The lemons in southern Italy are wonderful, so I use them whenever I can. This pudding is a beautiful colour, very fresh-looking, and can be set off brilliantly with a dusting of icing sugar and a few fresh berries.

SERVES 6–8

75 g/3 oz/⅓ cup butter, plus extra for greasing

225 g/8 oz/1 cup caster (superfine) sugar

Grated zest and juice of 3 lemons

3 eggs, separated

50 g/2 oz/½ cup self-raising (self-rising) flour

250 ml/8 fl oz/1 cup milk

30 ml/2 tbsp icing (confectioners') sugar

A few fresh berries, for decorating

1 Preheat the oven to 180°C/350°F/gas 4/fan oven 160°C and grease a 1 litre/1¾ pt/4¼ cup soufflé dish.

2 Cream together the butter and caster sugar and beat until pale and creamy.

3 Add the lemon zest, then gradually beat in one egg yolk at a time, adding a little of the flour and beating well if the mixture begins to curdle.

4 Blend in the flour and milk alternately until the mixture is smooth. Pour in the lemon juice and mix again to give a fairly runny mixture.

5 Whisk the egg whites until stiff, then gently fold into the lemon mixture and pour into the prepared soufflé dish.

6 Place the dish into a large baking tin (pan) and add enough boiling water to come half-way up the sides of the dish. Bake in the oven for 40–50 minutes until well risen and golden brown.

7 Remove from the oven and dust with icing sugar. Serve decorated with some fresh berries.

Hints and variations You can also serve this in individual ramekins (custard cups). You will need to shorten the cooking time a little.

Chocolate mousse with rum

This popular mousse is so rich that a little goes a long way. I find that an espresso cup is just the right amount for most people. You can leave out the rum if you prefer, but it does add that little something! See photograph opposite page 120.

SERVES 6–8

250 g/9 oz/1¾ cups good-quality plain (semi-sweet) chocolate

5 ml/1 tsp Mount Gay rum

4 egg whites

100 ml/3½ fl oz/scant ½ cup double (heavy) cream

30 ml/2 tbsp icing (confectioners') sugar

1 Grate about 75 g/3 oz/¾ cup of the chocolate and set aside.

2 Place the remaining chocolate in a bowl over a pan of hot water, without letting the water touch the bottom of the bowl. Melt the chocolate slowly, reheating the water if necessary.

3 Add the rum, which should thicken the mixture, then leave to cool.

4 Whisk the egg whites until firm but not solid. In a separate bowl, whisk the cream until stiff enough to form soft peaks. Fold the egg whites and cream into the chocolate.

5 Reserve 20 ml/4 tsp of the grated chocolate, then fold the remainder into the mousse.

6 Spoon the mixture into espresso cups, then sprinkle with the reserved grated chocolate. Cover and chill in the fridge for at least 4 hours.

7 Dust with icing sugar before serving.

Hints and variations Onboard the yachts the preferred rum is Mount Gay, which is produced on the island of Barbados in the Caribbean, but you can always adapt the recipe by using orange liqueur instead of rum. It's best to use good-quality plain chocolate with at least 70 per cent cocoa solids.

Orange tiramisu

Presented in a glass dish, the colourful layers of sponge, orange, chocolate and Mascarpone cheese look fabulous. Alternatively, you can make this tiramisu in individual glasses – great for a dinner party.

SERVES 6–8

1 double espresso coffee

30 ml/2 tbsp orange liqueur

2 oranges

400 ml/14 fl oz/1¾ cups Mascarpone cheese

2 egg yolks

30 ml/2 tbsp icing (confectioners') sugar

4 egg whites

1 box of sponge (lady) fingers, about 25 in total

225 g/8 oz/2 cups good-quality plain (semi-sweet) chocolate, grated and chilled

1 Mix the coffee and orange liqueur in a shallow dish.

2 Grate the zest from the oranges, then peel them. Holding the oranges over a bowl to catch the juice and using a very sharp knife, cut away the membrane to release the orange segments without any membrane or white pith. Break up the segments and put them in the bowl with the juice.

3 Beat the Mascarpone until soft, then beat in the egg yolks and icing sugar.

4 Whisk the egg whites until stiff, then fold them into the Mascarpone mixture with the orange zest.

5 Dip half the sponge fingers into the coffee mixture and make a layer in the bottom of a shallow glass dish. Lay half the orange segments on the sponge fingers and cover with a third of the grated chocolate. Gently spoon half the Mascarpone mixture on top and spread over evenly. Repeat the layers, finishing with the Mascarpone. Spread evenly, making sure you seal the edges, and sprinkle with the remaining grated chocolate.

6 Cover and chill overnight, if possible, before serving.

Hints and variations I make several variations on this fruit tiramisu, using strawberries, or almonds with amaretto liqueur or just the traditional one with plenty of grated chocolate.

Peach mousse in peach halves

Fresh peaches are sold in trays along the roads in southern Italy during late July and August. They are at their best at this time of the year in the Mediterranean, sun-ripened and so sweet and delicious.

SERVES 6–8

6 peaches

250 g/9 oz amaretto biscuits (cookies), crushed

15 ml/1 tbsp Marsala or sweet sherry

2 eggs, separated

30 ml/2 tbsp icing (confectioners') sugar

A few sprigs of fresh mint

1 Preheat the oven to 180°C/350°F/gas 4/fan oven 160°C.

2 Halve the peaches and carefully remove the stones (pits). Scoop out most of the flesh, leaving a thin layer in the skins.

3 Place the flesh in a bowl and mash, then stir in the crushed biscuits and Marsala or sherry.

4 Beat the egg yolks and add them to the peach mixture. Whisk the egg whites until stiff, then fold them in.

5 Arrange the peach shells in a baking tin (pan) and spoon in the mixture. Bake in the oven for 25 minutes until well risen and golden.

6 Arrange on individual plates, dust with icing sugar and decorate with sprigs of mint.

Serving suggestions I like to serve the peaches with a little single (light) pouring cream.

Hints and variations You can use peaches or nectarines for this recipe.

Mediterranean flavour There are so many different kinds of peaches and nectarines available in the Mediterranean: red, white, large, small and flat – and all, of course, full of juice and flavour. They are delicious simply poached with vanilla and cinnamon.

Panna cotta with strawberry coulis

The name of this traditional Italian dish means 'cooked cream'. It is delicious plain, or you can combine it with chocolate, coffee or almost any kind of fruit. In the Caribbean I use mangos or pineapples; in the Mediterranean I use the local fruits in season.

SERVES 6–8

250 ml/8 fl oz/1 cup water

225 g/8 oz/1 cup caster (superfine) sugar

225 g/8 oz strawberries

10 ml/2 tsp powdered gelatine or 12 leaves of gelatine

30 ml/2 tbsp water

750 ml/1¼ pts/3 cups double (heavy) cream

120 ml/4 fl oz/½ cup clear honey

1 vanilla pod

1 To make the coulis, put the water and sugar in a saucepan and heat through slowly until all the sugar has dissolved. Do not let it boil rapidly.

2 Reserve a few strawberries for decoration, then add the remaining fruit to the syrup and heat through for a few minutes. Rub the fruit through a sieve (strainer) to remove most of the seeds. Allow to cool.

3 To make the panna cotta, put the gelatine in a small bowl with the water. Stand the bowl in a pan of warm water until the gelatine has dissolved.

4 Bring the cream and honey to the boil in a heavy-based saucepan, then add the vanilla pod. Stir until well combined. Remove from the heat and stir in the gelatine.

5 Scrape out some of the vanilla seeds into the cream, then sieve the cream into six to eight ramekin dishes (custard cups).

6 Place in the fridge for at least 4 hours to chill and set.

7 Dip the ramekins quickly into hot water, then invert them on to individual plates. Surround with the fruit coulis and decorate with the reserved fruit.

Serving suggestions You can also serve panna cotta in wine glasses with some coulis on top.

Hints and variations You can use 100 g/4 oz/½ cup caster sugar instead of the honey, if you prefer.

Strawberry tart

This dessert is a wonderful dish to serve at the end of a light summer meal. You can make the pastry or use ready-made if you prefer – chilled or frozen pastry is excellent quality and saves time.

SERVES 6–8

450 g/1 lb sweet shortcrust pastry (basic pie crust)

1 egg, beaten

50 g/2 oz/½ cup ground almonds

225 g/8 oz/1 cup caster (superfine) sugar

30 ml/2 tbsp plain (all-purpose) flour

900 g/2 lb strawberries, hulled, and halved if large

30 ml/2 tbsp icing (confectioners') sugar

1 Roll out the pastry (paste) on a lightly floured surface and use two-thirds to line a 23 cm/9 in flan dish. Roll out the remaining pastry to a 23 cm/9 in circle and cut with a lattice cutter. Alternatively, roll out and cut into strips so that you can make a lattice on the top of the tart. Chill for 30 minutes.

2 Preheat the oven to 180°C/350°F/gas 4/fan oven 160°C.

3 Cover the pastry case (pie shell) with greaseproof (waxed) paper and fill with baking beans. Bake blind for 10 minutes, then remove the beans and paper and brush the pastry with beaten egg. Return to the oven for 5 minutes, then remove from the oven and leave to cool slightly.

4 Sprinkle the ground almonds over the bottom of the pastry case.

5 Mix together the caster sugar and flour. Toss the strawberries in the mixture, then arrange them in the pastry case. Top with the lattice pastry, dampening the edges with beaten egg and sealing them well. Brush the top with egg.

6 Bake in the oven for 35 minutes until the pastry is golden and crisp.

7 Allow to cool before serving dusted with the icing sugar.

Serving suggestions Serve with fresh cream or ice cream. A sprig of mint and a few fresh strawberries will add to the presentation.

Mediterranean flavour The strawberry season is one of my favourite times in the Mediterranean; the berries are so sweet and just melt in your mouth. I buy trays of them in the market and make strawberry jam (conserve) and lots of coulis, which I freeze. I also freeze the strawberries themselves so that I can make strawberry daiquiris at any time of year!

Apple tarts with ground almonds and marmalade

Individual tarts are so much more personal than slices from a large one. Although they do take a bit longer to prepare, I think it's worth it.

SERVES 6–8

400 g/14 oz sweet shortcrust pastry (basic pie crust)

900 g/2 lb cooking (tart) apples

100 g/4 oz/½ cup caster (superfine) sugar

Juice of 2 oranges

Grated zest of 1 lemon

50 g/2 oz/½ cup ground almonds

A squeeze of lemon juice

175 g/6 oz/½ cup orange marmalade

1 Preheat the oven to 180°C/350°F/gas 4/fan oven 160°C.

2 Roll out the pastry (paste) on a lightly floured surface and use to line six to eight individual flan dishes. Chill for 30 minutes.

3 Cover the pastry cases (pie shells) with greaseproof (waxed) paper and fill with baking beans. Bake in the oven for 10 minutes, then remove the paper and beans.

4 Peel, core and chop a third of the apples and place them in a pan with the sugar and orange juice. Slowly bring to the boil, then reduce the heat and simmer for about 10 minutes until soft, stirring regularly to make sure they do not stick to the pan. Add the lemon zest and almonds. Taste the fruit and add a little more sugar if it is a bit sharp.

5 Peel and core the remaining apples, then slice them thinly into a bowl of water to which you have added a squeeze of lemon juice. This will stop them from going brown.

6 Spoon the apple sauce into the pastry cases. Drain the apple slices, then arrange them attractively on the top. Bake in the oven for 20–30 minutes until golden brown.

7 While the tarts are cooking, gently warm the marmalade and sieve it to remove any lumps. Brush the tops of the hot flans generously with the marmalade. Serve hot, warm or cool.

Serving suggestions A swirl of cream, a dollop of crème fraîche or a scoop of vanilla ice cream all make perfect accompaniments to these tarts.

Hints and variations Don't chill this before serving – if it is too cold it will mask the flavour.

If you can't get ready-made sweet shortcrust pastry, the cheat's trick is to use plain but roll it out using icing sugar instead of flour to provide the desired sweetness.

Apricot tarte tatin

The traditional tarte tatin uses apple – but I think my version is even better! The rich golden colour of this dish is created by caramelising the fruit and juices. I always make it when I can buy fresh apricots in the market.

SERVES 6

100 g/4 oz/½ cup caster (superfine) sugar

120 ml/4 fl oz/½ cup water

450 g/1 lb fresh apricots, halved and stoned (pitted)

Butter for greasing

250 g/9 oz/1 packet of puff pastry (paste)

1 Preheat the oven to 180°C/350°F/gas 4/fan oven 160°C.

2 Dissolve the sugar in the water in a saucepan. Add the apricots and simmer very gently for about 10 minutes until soft.

3 Arrange the apricots cut-sides down in the bottom of a greased 20 cm/8 in ovenproof flan dish and pour the cooking syrup over the top.

4 Roll out the pastry on a lightly floured surface and cut it to fit the dish. Place it on top of the apricots, pressing down gently. Cut an air hole in the centre of the pastry. Bake in the oven for 35–40 minutes until well risen and golden brown.

5 Remove the tart from the oven and allow to cool for 30 minutes. Loosen the edges and invert it on to a large plate, making sure all the apricots and juices come out with the pastry.

6 Serve warm or cool, not chilled.

Serving suggestions This is delicious with chilled fresh cream or vanilla ice cream.

Plum tart with puff pastry

Plums are in the markets in the Mediterranean from early summer onwards. Sliced and dusted with icing sugar, this colourful tart is great either served warm from the oven or left to cool. I use frozen puff pastry.

SERVES 8

300 g/11 oz puff pastry (paste)

60 ml/4 tbsp milk, plus extra for brushing

175 g/6 oz/1 cup semolina (cream of wheat)

450 g/1 lb plums, stoned (pitted) and sliced

100 g/4 oz/1 cup flaked (slivered) almonds

30 ml/2 tbsp clear honey

30 ml/2 tbsp icing (confectioners') sugar

1 Roll out the pastry on a lightly floured surface and cut it into a rectangle about 20 x 30 cm/8 x 12 in. Cut a 'frame' 2.5 cm/1 in wide all round the edges of the rectangle and carefully lift it away. Roll the remaining pastry again so that it is restored to the original size and place it on a dampened baking (cookie) sheet. Brush the edges with a little of the milk, then position the frame on top and press down lightly. Score the frame diagonally all the way round. Chill for 30 minutes.

2 Preheat the oven to 180°C/350°F/gas 4/fan oven 160°C.

3 Scatter the semolina over the base of the pastry, then arrange the plum slices evenly over the top. Brush the pastry frame with milk. Bake in the oven for 25–30 minutes until the pastry is risen and golden brown.

4 Toast the almonds for a few minutes in a dry frying pan (skillet), tossing until just golden. Remove from the pan.

5 Once the tart is cooked, drizzle the honey over the plums and sprinkle with the toasted almonds. Dust with the icing sugar before serving.

Serving suggestions Serve warm or cold with cream, ice cream or crème fraîche.

Hints and variations Apricots or pears are a great alternative to the plums and go perfectly with the pastry, honey and nuts.

Fruit flan with mascarpone

Mascarpone, Italian cream cheese, is wonderful for this dessert as it holds so well with the berries on top. Made as a large flan, it looks very impressive when presented at a summer dinner or lunch party.

SERVES 6–8

450 g/1 lb sweet shortcrust pastry (basic pie crust)

400 g/14 oz mixed berries such as strawberries, raspberries, blueberries and blackberries

75 g/3 oz/⅓ cup icing (confectioners') sugar

300 ml/½ pt/1¼ cups Mascarpone cheese

5 ml/1 tsp vanilla essence (extract)

Grated zest of 1 lemon

2 egg whites

2.5 ml/½ tsp powdered gelatine OR 1 leaf of gelatine

30 ml/2 tbsp raspberry coulis (see page 121)

A few fresh mint leaves

Photograph opposite:
Chocolate Mousse with Rum (see page 112)

1 Roll out the pastry (paste) on a lightly floured surface and use to line a 23–25 cm/9–10 in flan tin (pie pan). Chill for 30 minutes.

2 Preheat the oven to 180°C/350°F/gas 4/fan oven 160°C.

3 Cover the pastry with greaseproof (waxed) paper, fill with baking beans and bake blind for 15 minutes until the pastry is lightly golden. Remove the paper and beans and allow to cool.

4 Chop half the fruit and place in a bowl with 15 ml/1 tbsp of the icing sugar.

5 Beat the remaining icing sugar into the Mascarpone with the vanilla essence and lemon zest. Whisk the egg whites until stiff, then fold them into the Mascarpone. Carefully fold in the chopped fruit.

6 Spoon the Mascarpone mixture into the pastry case (pie shell) and arrange the whole berries on the top.

7 Dissolve the powdered gelatine in a little water, then add it to the coulis. If you are using a gelatine leaf, warm it in the fruit coulis until it dissolves, then leave to cool slightly. Pour the coulis over the tart and decorate with the mint leaves.

8 Chill until ready to serve.

Hints and variations Try making this with just one fruit or just red fruits rather than mixed fruits. You can also make it in individual flan cases.

If you do not want to use a coulis with gelatine for the glaze, you can heat 4 large tablespoonfuls of raspberry jam (conserve), then sieve (strain) it and brush over the berries. Allow it to cool before serving.

If you can't get ready-made sweet shortcrust pastry, the cheat's trick is to use plain but roll it out using icing sugar instead of flour to provide the desired sweetness.

Puff pastry fruit stacks with fruit coulis and vanilla cream

There are several elements to this dish, which you simply bring together at the last minute to make a colourful centrepiece on a dessert plate. You can use one fruit or several and can cut the pastry into different shapes. Serve with a glass of champagne.

SERVES 6–8

FOR THE MARINATED FRUIT
200 g/7 oz raspberries

200 g/7 oz blueberries

450 ml/³/₄ pint/2 cups champagne or sparkling wine

300 g/11 oz puff pastry (paste)

Icing (confectioners') sugar for dusting

FOR THE RASPBERRY COULIS
200 g/7 oz raspberries

100 g/4 oz/²/₃ cup icing sugar

Juice of ¹/₂ lemon

FOR THE VANILLA CREAM
250 g/9 oz/generous 1 cup Mascarpone cheese

75 g/3 oz/¹/₃ cup icing sugar

2 drops of vanilla essence (extract)

2 egg whites, beaten

1 To make the marinated fruit, place half the raspberries and all the blueberries in a bowl with the champagne or sparkling wine. Place this and the remainder of the fruit in the fridge to chill.

2 Roll out the pastry on a lightly floured surface to about 5 mm/¹/₄ in thick. Cut out 24 pastry shapes using a shaped cutter to make circles, stars, hearts or whatever you like. Arrange the shapes on dampened baking (cookie) sheets, prick them all over with a fork and chill for 30 minutes.

3 Preheat the oven to 180°C/350°F/gas 4/fan oven 160°C.

4 Bake in the oven for 10–15 minutes until the pastry is golden. Remove from the oven and dust a third of the shapes with a little icing sugar. Leave to cool.

5 To make the coulis, put the raspberries, icing sugar and lemon juice in a pan, bring gently to the boil, then reduce the heat and simmer until the sugar has melted, stirring occasionally. Simmer for a further few minutes until the raspberries are soft. Remove from the heat and rub through a metal sieve (strainer). Leave to cool, then chill.

6 To make the vanilla cream, beat the Mascarpone with the icing sugar and vanilla essence until it forms stiff peaks. Fold in the beaten egg whites. Cover and chill.

7 When you are ready to serve, drain the champagne off the fruit (but don't waste the champagne!). Place one of the unsugared pastry shapes on each plate and top with a spoonful of the vanilla cream, then marinated fruit and a little more of the cream. Place a second unsugared pastry shape on top, then cream, marinated fruit and more cream. Finally, top with the sugared pastry shapes. Pour some coulis around the stacks and decorate with the reserved raspberries.

Photograph opposite:
Plum Cake with Ginger and Cinnamon
(see page 136)

Strawberries and cream cheese in filo pastry

These look fabulous stacked on white plates and dusted with a little icing sugar, so that the contrast of colours shows. If strawberries aren't available you could use other fruits and I've given some suggestions below.

SERVES 6

20 fresh strawberries, hulled

30 ml/2 tbsp caster (superfine) sugar

Grated zest of 1 lemon

225 g/8 oz/1 cup full-fat soft cream cheese

3 sheets of filo pastry (paste)

100 g/4 oz/½ cup butter, melted

Icing (confectioners') sugar for dusting

A few fresh mint leaves, to decorate

1 Cut half the strawberries into small pieces and set aside.

2 Whisk the sugar and lemon zest into the cream cheese, then fold in the strawberry pieces.

3 Cover the sheets of filo you are not using with a damp tea towel (dish cloth) to prevent them from drying out. Take one sheet of filo and cut it in half lengthways to give two strips, each about 7.5 x 20 cm/3 x 8 in. Lay one strip on the work surface and brush the edges with melted butter. Place a small spoonful of the cream cheese mixture on one end. Fold the corner of the pastry over to form a triangle, then continue to fold the strip over and over the triangle shape, sealing the edges gently. Repeat with the remaining pastry. Arrange the triangles on a greased baking (cookie) sheet and chill for 30 minutes.

4 Preheat the oven to 180°C/350°F/gas 4/fan oven 160°C.

5 Bake the strawberry triangles for 20–30 minutes until golden brown.

6 Dust the parcels generously with icing sugar and serve on individual plates with the reserved strawberries and the mint leaves.

Hints and variations Raspberries, blueberries or blackberries work just as well for this dish. Peaches can also work very well. Skin them before dicing and mixing in with the cream cheese.

Key lime pie

The recipe was actually given to me while sailing in the Caribbean. The locals there often add a drop of green food colouring to the condensed milk but I prefer to avoid food colourings on the whole.

SERVES 6–8

300 g/11 oz sweet shortcrust pastry (basic pie crust)

350 ml/12 fl oz/1⅓ cups unsweetened condensed milk

4 eggs, separated

225 g/8 oz/1 cup caster (superfine) sugar

Grated zest and juice of 4 limes

1 Preheat the oven to 180°C/350°F/gas 4/fan oven 160°C.

2 Roll out the pastry (paste) on a lightly floured surface and use to line a 23–25 cm/9–10 in flan tin (pie pan). Chill for 30 minutes.

3 Cover the pastry with greaseproof (waxed) paper, fill with baking beans and bake blind for 10 minutes. Remove the paper and beans and bake for a further 5 minutes, then allow to cool.

4 Whisk together the condensed milk and egg yolks, then gradually add two-thirds of the sugar until well blended. Whisk in the lime zest and juice. Pour into the baked flan case (pie shell) and bake in the oven for 10–15 minutes.

5 Whisk the egg whites until they are softly peaking. Add the remaining sugar and whisk until stiff and glossy.

6 Spoon the egg white on the top of the cooked flan, sealing it carefully against the pastry edges. Return to the oven for a further 10 minutes until the topping is just golden.

7 Serve warm or cold.

Hints and variations Use lemons instead of limes for a lemon meringue pie. Make sure you watch the meringue while it is cooking as it can easily burn.

If you can't get ready-made sweet shortcrust pastry, the cheat's trick is to use plain but roll it out using icing sugar instead of flour to provide the desired sweetness.

Caramelised fresh peaches

Fresh sun-ripened peaches are wonderful in August throughout the Mediterranean, with their superb juicy flesh and intoxicating aroma. Peaches for this recipe should be ripe but still firm, as they contain the most sugar then and caramelise well.

SERVES 6–8

100 g/4 oz/½ cup caster (superfine) sugar

120 ml/4 fl oz/½ cup water

30 ml/2 tbsp Marsala or sweet sherry

6 ripe peaches, halved and stoned (pitted)

30 ml/2 tbsp soft brown sugar

1 Warm the caster sugar and water in a large saucepan until the sugar has dissolved. Bring to the boil, then reduce the heat to a simmer.

2 Add the Marsala or sherry. Place the peaches cut-sides down in the sugar syrup and cook for 4 minutes. Turn the peaches over and cook for about a further 4 minutes until soft.

3 Lift the peaches on to a grill (broiler) pan and sprinkle with the brown sugar. Grill (broil) for 5 minutes until the sugar has caramelised.

4 Serve hot or cold.

Serving suggestions Accompany with cream, Mascarpone Cream (see below) or scoops of ice cream.

Hints and variations You can use nectarines instead of peaches.

Mascarpone cream

This is such a useful staple: an easy-to-make cream that you can flavour with all sorts of things, from alcohol and fruit zests to vanilla or coffee flavouring. This quantity is sufficient to serve 6–8 guests as an accompaniment to desserts.

MAKES ABOUT 300 ML/½ PT/1¼ CUPS

250 ml/8 fl oz/1 cup Mascarpone cheese

30 ml/2 tbsp icing (confectioners') sugar

2.5 ml/½ tsp orange liqueur

Grated zest of 1 orange

1 Beat together all the ingredients. Taste and add a little more liqueur or sugar if you wish.

2 Chill in the fridge until ready to serve.

Lemon cheesecake with strawberries

*This is a fairly light cheesecake, which provides a delicious complement to the flavour
of summer strawberries, and a beautiful colour contrast too. I sometimes make this
as one large cheesecake and sometimes as individual ones.*

SERVES 6–8

**4 x 250 g/9 oz tubs of full-fat soft
cream cheese**

**100 g/4 oz/¹⁄₂ cup caster
(superfine) sugar**

4 eggs, separated

**250 ml/8 fl oz/1 cup double
(heavy) cream**

Grated zest of 4 lemons

1 Preheat the oven to 180°C/350°F/gas 4/fan oven 160°C and grease a
1.5 litre/2¹⁄₂ pt/6 cup soufflé dish.

2 Blend the cream cheese, sugar and egg yolks in a blender or food
processor, then add the cream and lemon zest. Pour into a large
bowl.

3 Whisk the egg whites until stiff, then fold into the cream cheese
mixture and pour into the prepared soufflé dish.

4 Place the soufflé dish in a large deep roasting tin (pan) and pour in
enough boiling water to come half-way up the sides of the soufflé
dish. Bake in the oven for 1¹⁄₂ hours. Keep an eye on the cheesecake
towards the end of cooking and cover with foil if it begins to brown
too much.

5 Turn off the oven and leave the cheesecake in the oven to cool with
the door ajar. Chill before serving.

Serving suggestions This makes a lovely accompaniment for fresh
summer fruit, such as strawberries.

Hints and variations Try making the cheesecake with orange zest
and juice instead of lemon.

Chocolate and nut meringue with apricot compôte

*The wonderful, slightly bitter taste of a good dessert chocolate contrasts perfectly
with the fresh flavour of the apricots and certainly doesn't overpower the dessert.
You could use peaches or nectarines too.*

126

SERVES 6–8

**350 g/12 oz stoned (pitted)
fresh apricots, sliced**

250 ml/8 fl oz/1 cup water

**350 g/12 oz/1½ cups caster
(superfine) sugar**

100 g/4 oz/1 cup almonds

50 g/2 oz/½ cup hazelnuts (filberts)

**50 g/2 oz/½ cup flaked (slivered)
almonds, toasted**

6 egg whites

A pinch of cream of tartar

**100 g/4 oz/1 cup good-quality plain
(semi-sweet) chocolate, chopped**

450 ml/¾ pt/2 cups whipping cream

1 Preheat the oven to 180°C/350°F/gas 4/fan oven 160°C and grease and line a 26 cm/10½ in springform cake tin (pan).

2 Place the apricots, water and 225 g/8 oz/1 cup of the sugar in a pan and heat gently until the sugar has dissolved. Bring the boil, then reduce the heat and simmer for 15 minutes until the liquid has reduced and the apricots are soft. Set aside to cool.

3 Toast the whole almonds in a dry pan for a few minutes until golden, then remove from the pan and divide in half. Toast the hazelnuts in the same way and mix with one half of the almonds, then grind coarsely.

4 Toast the flaked almonds and set aside.

5 Whisk the egg whites with the cream of tartar until almost stiff, then whisk in the remaining sugar until the mixture is silky and stiff. Gently fold in half the chopped chocolate and the ground nuts.

6 Spoon into the cake tin and bake in the oven for 1½ hours until the meringue is risen and golden brown. Allow to cool in the tin for 10 minutes, then transfer to a wire rack to finish cooling.

7 Whisk the cream until stiff, then fold in the reserved toasted almonds and the remaining chocolate. Gently fold in half the apricot compôte.

8 Place the meringue on a serving platter. Spoon over the apricot and cream mixture. Spoon the rest of the apricot compôte on top and then sprinkle over the flaked almonds.

Hints and variations If you can't get fresh apricots, use 250 g/9 oz/1½ cups ready-to-eat dried apricots, sliced.

Raspberries also work well in this recipe. You don't need to cook them, just macerate half of them in a little icing (confectioners') sugar, then fold them into the cream. Use the remainder fresh on top.

Crêpes suzettes

These crêpes are popular at any time of day. I always have some ready-made crêpes in the freezer as sometimes my guests like them for breakfast. I can then put together this dessert in minutes.

MAKES ABOUT 20

450 ml/³⁄₄ pt/2 cups milk

2 eggs

225 g/8 oz/2 cups plain (all-purpose) flour

A pinch of salt

25 g/1 oz/2 tbsp butter, melted

A little oil or butter, for cooking

Grated zest and juice of 2 oranges

120 ml/4 fl oz/¹⁄₂ cup orange juice

15 ml/1 tbsp icing (confectioners') sugar

225 g/8 oz/1 cup cold butter, diced

45 ml/3 tbsp brandy or orange liqueur

1 Whisk together the milk and eggs, then whisk in the flour and salt until smooth. Stir in the melted butter. Leave the mixture to stand for at least 30 minutes before using.

2 Heat a small crêpe pan until it is really hot and brush with a little oil or butter. Spoon in a little of the batter and swirl it over the base of the pan, then cook for a few minutes until golden on the underside. Flip over and cook the other side. Fold the pancake and keep warm while you continue to make the remaining pancakes in the same way.

3 Place the orange zest and juice in a saucepan and make up to 250 ml/8 fl oz/1 cup with the additional orange juice. Add the sugar and heat gently until dissolved, then gradually add the cold butter, one piece at a time, whisking continually until the sauce thickens. Stir in the brandy or orange liqueur.

4 Slide the pancakes through the sauce to coat, then serve on warm plates.

Serving suggestions I like to fold them and serve two on each plate, topped with a slice of orange and perhaps some fresh fruit coulis. Finally, for a really indulgent treat, serve with cream or crème fraîche. For breakfast, serve with slices of fresh apple tossed in a mixture of melted butter, sugar and cinnamon.

Hints and variations The first pancake never works properly, so be prepared to throw it away. Once the pan gets hot, you'll get into the swing of things!

Wholewheat pancakes with honey, figs and greek yoghurt

Wholemeal flour gives a deliciously nutty taste to this light and easy dessert, which also makes a perfect breakfast dish. It has a truly Mediterranean flavour that always makes me think of the hot Greek sunshine – even when it's cold and raining.

SERVES 6–8

2 eggs

450 ml/³/₄ pt/2 cups milk

175 g/6 oz/1½ cups wholemeal (wholewheat) flour

50 g/2 oz/½ cup plain (all-purpose) flour

30 ml/2 tbsp melted butter, plus extra for greasing

2.5 ml/½ tsp baking powder

A knob of butter

6–8 ripe figs, quartered

300 ml/½ pt/1¼ cups Greek yoghurt

350 g/12 oz/1 cup clear thyme or pine honey

15 ml/1 tbsp sesame seeds

1 Whisk together the eggs and milk, then whisk in the flours until smooth. Whisk in the melted butter and baking powder. Leave the mixture to stand for 30 minutes.

2 Heat a small crêpe pan until it is really hot and brush with a little melted butter. Spoon in a little of the batter and swirl it over the base of the pan, then cook for a few minutes until golden on the underside. Flip over and cook the other side. Continue until you have used all the batter and you have about 24 small pancakes. Fold the pancakes and keep them warm.

3 Add the knob of butter to the pan and fry (sauté) the fig quarters for a few minutes.

4 Arrange three or four pancakes and some fig pieces on each plate with a spoonful of Greek yoghurt, then drizzle with the honey and sprinkle with the sesame seeds just before serving.

Hints and variations You can use almost any fruits you like in this dish. Try fresh apricots, nectarines, peaches or soft berries. You can also omit the wholewheat flour and use just plain flour if you prefer.

The quantity of pancake mixture allows for one or two failures!

Baked pineapple with coconut ice cream

*This dish is easy to make but you do need to prepare the ice cream in the morning
so it has time to freeze. For a special occasion, I peel and core mini-pineapples –
they look so stunning when coated in the sugar syrup and baked whole.*

SERVES 6–8

2 large pineapples

**100 g/4 oz/½ cup caster (superfine)
sugar**

120 ml/4 fl oz/½ cup water

FOR THE ICE CREAM
100 g/4 oz/½ cup caster sugar

**250 ml/8 fl oz/1 cup double (heavy)
cream**

**30 ml/2 tbsp unsweetened desiccated
(shredded) coconut**

**400 ml/14 fl oz/1 large can of creamed
coconut**

A few fresh mint leaves, to decorate

1 Preheat the oven to 150°C/300°F/gas 2/fan oven 135°C.

2 Peel the pineapples and slice thinly through the whole pineapple.
Arrange the slices in baking tins (pans).

3 Dissolve the sugar in the water over a low heat, then boil for
5 minutes to make a syrup. Brush over the pineapple slices, then
bake in the oven for 50 minutes. Turn them over and bake for a
further 30–50 minutes until golden brown, checking every now and
then so that they do not burn towards the end of cooking. Transfer
to a wire rack to cool.

4 To make the ice cream, dissolve the sugar in the cream over a gentle
heat, then stir in the desiccated coconut and creamed coconut and
leave to cool. If you have an ice cream maker, churn until ready, then
place in a freezer container and freeze. If not, place in a freezer
container and freeze for 1 hour, then break it up with a fork and
freeze again. Repeat this three times, then leave the ice cream to
freeze completely.

5 Arrange the pineapple slices on individual plates with a couple of
scoops of ice cream and serve decorated with mint leaves.

Serving suggestions For special occasions, I break coconuts in half
to make bowls that I fill with the ice cream, then push in the
pineapple slices like wafer biscuits. I sometimes drizzle some
passion fruit pulp over the top – stunning!

Hints and variations You can store the baked pineapple slices in an
airtight container for a few days if you want to make them in
advance.

Crisp won ton leaves with plums and mascarpone

Won tons are great to use in all sorts of ways. Here I just deep-fry them and use them as crisp wafers, giving a great contrast of tastes and textures of the plums and Mascarpone in this dish.

SERVES 6–8

500 g/18 oz plums, halved and stoned (pitted)

100 g/4 oz/½ cup caster (superfine) sugar

120 ml/4 fl oz/½ cup orange juice

Grated zest of 1 orange

250 g/9 oz/1 packet of won ton wrappers

Groundnut (peanut) oil, for cooking

175 g/6 oz/1 cup icing (confectioners') sugar, plus extra for dusting

250 ml/8 fl oz/1 cup Mascarpone cheese

1 Put the plums, caster sugar, orange juice and zest in a saucepan, bring to the boil, then reduce the heat and simmer gently for about 10 minutes until the plums are soft. Set aside to cool.

2 Cut the won tons into 6–7.5 cm/2½–3 in rounds using a pastry (cookie) cutter or by cutting round a cup. You need about 24 circles.

3 Heat a little oil in a frying pan (skillet) and cook the won tons for a few minutes until golden, watching carefully so that they do not burn. Drain on kitchen paper (paper towels) and dust with a little icing sugar.

4 Mix the measured icing sugar with the Mascarpone until smooth and stiff. Chill for at least 20 minutes.

5 Place a won ton on a plate, spoon some plums into the centre and top with a spoonful of Mascarpone and another won ton. Add two more layers of won tons and Mascarpone.

6 Drizzle some of the plum juices over and around the plate and serve.

Hints and variations If you want to use another fruit, try stewing some fresh or dried apricots, or use fresh peaches. If you cannot get won ton wrappers, brush squares of filo pastry with groundnut oil, layer two or three together and bake them instead.

A 250 g/9 oz packet contains about 80 wrappers, which is far more than you need – I just take out what I need and then return the packet to the freezer.

Limoncello

This sweet Italian liqueur comes from Sorrento and is also known as limoncino. The recipe was given to me by an English friend who has lived in Viareggio for about 12 years. We enjoy it ice cold from the freezer as a shot or as a long drink with soda water.

SERVES 8

6 large unwaxed lemons

750 ml/1¼ pts/3 cups vodka

750 ml/1¼ pts/3 cups water

700 g/1½ lb/3 cups caster (superfine) sugar

1 Wash the lemons very thoroughly, then peel them very finely using a potato peeler, avoiding the white pith. Put the vodka and the peel in an airtight container and leave for 24 hours.

2 Mix the water and sugar together in a saucepan and heat gently until the sugar dissolves. Bring to the boil and boil for 5 minutes to make a syrup. Leave to cool.

3 Add the alcohol and lemon rind and leave to infuse for 30 minutes. Strain into bottles, seal and label.

4 Place in the freezer for an hour or so before serving.

Hints and variations You can also use the skins of oranges or other citrus fruits to make similar drinks, or some people also make it with strawberries.

Mediterranean flavour This drink is found all over Italy but the best comes from the area around Naples, where the most succulent lemons grow in abundance.

cakes and bakes

I bake most days when I am on the boat. When there are small children around, I like to let them join in the preparation, rolling out and cutting the cookies. I have to keep a sharp look-out to make sure not too much of the mixture ends up in their mouths! Since the yachts are always rocking about, I prefer to use an oven that is mounted on a gimbal, which keeps it level. That way I can make sure my cakes and bakes come out flat rather than like door wedges!

Orange and almond cake

This is a deliciously moist cake that will last for several days if kept in an airtight container – though I've never known it remain untouched that long! You can serve it as a dessert or with coffee.

SERVES 6–8

2 oranges

250 g/9 oz/2¼ cups ground almonds

4 eggs

100 g/4 oz/½ cup caster (superfine) sugar

10 ml/2 tsp baking powder

15 ml/1 tbsp icing (confectioners') sugar

1 Preheat the oven to 180°C/350°F/gas 4/fan oven 160°C and grease and flour a 24 cm/9½ in springform cake tin (pan).

2 Place the oranges in a saucepan, cover with water and bring to the boil. Boil for about 40 minutes until the skins of the oranges are soft. Allow to cool.

3 Cut the oranges into quarters and remove the core, peel, pith and membranes. Place the flesh in a blender or food processor and chop roughly. Add the ground almonds, eggs, sugar and baking powder.

4 Pour the mixture into the prepared tin and bake in the centre of the oven for 50–60 minutes until a knife inserted in the centre comes out clean. Check the cake after 20 minutes and cover with greased foil if it is browning too quickly.

5 Turn out on to a wire rack to cool, then dust with the icing sugar before serving.

Serving suggestions Slice the cake and serve it with a dollop of whipped cream on the side. Alternatively, slice it horizontally through the middle and fill with a layer of Mascarpone Cream (see page 124).

Hints and variations I sometimes make a sugar syrup with 100 g/ 4 oz/1 cup of sugar and 375 ml/13 fl oz/1½ cups of water, simmered until the sugar has melted. Pour it over the warm cake and allow it to soak in before serving. If you make the cake with a cream filling, remember to store it in the fridge.

Lemon rice cake

A light, deliciously lemony cake, this tastes just as good whether you eat it warm from the oven or after it has cooled to room temperature. Using rice in cakes is in the traditional Italian style.

SERVES 6–8

50 g/2 oz/½ cup ground almonds

450 g/1 lb/2 cups round-grain (pudding) rice

225 g/8 oz/1 cup caster (superfine) sugar

450 ml/¾ pt/2 cups milk

Grated rind and juice of 2 lemons

3 eggs, separated

A pinch of cream of tartar

Icing (confectioners') sugar, for dusting

1 Preheat the oven to 180°C/350°F/gas 4/fan oven 160°C. Grease a 26 cm/10½ in springform cake tin (pan) and sprinkle in about half the ground almonds, tipping to coat the base and sides.

2 Place the rice in a bag and crush the grains roughly with a rolling pin.

3 Place the crushed rice, sugar and milk in a saucepan and bring to the boil, then reduce the heat and simmer gently for about 10 minutes until all the milk has been absorbed, stirring regularly so the rice does not stick or burn. Allow to cool slightly.

4 Stir in the lemon juice, rind and remaining ground almonds.

5 Beat the egg yolks, then stir them into the rice.

6 Whisk the egg whites and cream of tartar until stiff, then fold into the rice mixture. Spoon into the prepared tin and level the top.

7 Bake in the oven for 35–40 minutes until golden brown. Leave to cool in the tin for 10 minutes, then turn out and leave to cool on a wire rack.

8 Dust with icing sugar before serving.

Serving suggestions Serve with cream and a bowl of fresh berries or some raspberry or other fruit coulis (see page 121).

Flourless chocolate cake

This chocolate cake goes down well with everyone, including people who say they are on diets, don't eat desserts or can't eat another thing! It is crunchy on the outside, soft and moist on the inside and very rich.

SERVES 6–8

225 g/8 oz/2 cups good-quality plain (semi-sweet) chocolate, broken into pieces

225 g/8 oz/1 cup butter, diced

4 eggs, separated

225 g/8 oz/1 cup caster (superfine) sugar

15 ml/1 tbsp icing (confectioners') sugar

1 Preheat the oven to 180°C/350°F/gas 4/fan oven 160°C and grease a deep 20 cm/8 in loose-bottomed cake tin (pan).

2 Melt the chocolate in a bowl over a pan of gently simmering water, making sure that you do not let the water touch the bottom of the bowl. Add the butter and stir until the mixture is smooth. Remove from the heat.

3 Whisk together the egg yolks and half the sugar until thick and pale. Beat into the chocolate mixture, making sure it is well blended.

4 Whisk the egg whites until they form soft peaks, then add the remaining sugar and whisk until the mixture is soft and smooth with firm peaks. Fold a third gently into the chocolate mixture to loosen the mixture, then very gently fold in the remaining egg white, keeping in as much air as possible.

5 Pour into the prepared tin and bake in the oven for 40 minutes until well risen and springy to the touch. A skewer inserted in the centre should come out clean. Leave to cool in the tin for 10 minutes, then turn out to finish cooling on a wire rack. Be prepared for the cake to sink and crack – that's what's supposed to happen.

6 Dust with the icing sugar before serving.

Serving suggestions Cut the cake into slices and serve with fresh berries and a little whipped or pouring cream.

Plum cake with ginger and cinnamon

I have to try and hide this cake while it is cooling as it is very popular with the crew and tends to 'disappear' when I am not looking! It has a lovely moist texture and a beautiful flavour. See photograph opposite page 121.

SERVES 6–8

225 g/8 oz/1 cup caster (superfine) sugar

150 g/5 oz/²⁄₃ cup butter, softened

3 eggs, beaten

5 ml/1 tsp vanilla essence (extract)

Grated zest of 1 lemon

200 g/7 oz/1¾ cups self-raising (self-rising) flour

5 ml/1 tsp baking powder

2.5 ml/½ tsp ground ginger

5 ml/1 tsp cinnamon

45 ml/3 tbsp milk

6–8 plums, stoned (pitted) and sliced

1 Preheat the oven to 180°C/350°F/gas 4/fan oven 160°C and grease and line a 24 cm/9½ in springform cake tin (pan).

2 Reserve 5 ml/1 tsp of the sugar for the topping, then beat the remainder with the butter until light and fluffy. Gradually add the beaten eggs. Beat in the vanilla essence and lemon zest.

3 Mix together the flour, baking powder, ginger and half the cinnamon, then fold into the mixture. Add the milk to form a light doughy consistency.

4 Mix half the plum slices into the dough, then spoon it into the prepared tin. Scatter the rest of the plums on top.

5 Bake in the oven for 50–60 minutes until well risen and firm. Check half way through cooking and cover loosely with buttered foil if it appears to be browning too quickly.

6 Remove from the oven. Mix the remaining sugar and cinnamon and sprinkle over the top of the warm cake. Leave to cool in the tin for 30 minutes, then turn out on to a wire rack and leave to cool completely before serving.

Hints and variations Other fruits such as pears, apricots or apples work really well in this recipe. Slice them thinly and add half to the mixture and layer the remainder on the top of the cake before baking.

Sugar cookies

This is a great base for any number of different-flavoured treats. See the note below for some suggestions. The dough will keep in the freezer for up to a month, so you can always have some freshly baked cookies whenever you want them.

MAKES 15–20

150 g/5 oz/²⁄₃ cup butter

150 g/5 oz/²⁄₃ cup caster (superfine) sugar

1 egg, beaten

30 ml/2 tbsp milk

5 ml/1 tsp vanilla essence (extract)

350 g/12 oz/3 cups plain (all-purpose) flour

5 ml/1 tsp baking powder

1 Beat together the butter and sugar until pale and fluffy. Beat the egg with the milk and vanilla essence.

2 Add the egg mixture to the butter mixture, a little at a time, beating well between each addition. When the mixture starts to become loose or looks as though it might curdle, begin to add the flour and baking powder a little at a time, continuing until you have a thick and kneadable dough. You may not need all the flour as you do not want the mixture to be too dry.

3 Turn out on to a lightly floured surface and knead gently for a few minutes, then wrap in clingfilm (plastic wrap) and chill for 30 minutes.

4 Preheat the oven to 180°C/350°F/gas 4/fan oven 160°C and grease a large baking (cookie) sheet.

5 Roll out the dough on a lightly floured surface to about 5–10 mm/ ¼–½ in thick and cut into shapes with biscuit (cookie) cutters. Place on the baking sheet and bake in the oven for 8–10 minutes until lightly golden but still slightly soft. Use a slice to transfer them carefully to a wire rack to finish cooling and hardening.

Hints and variations I use various cutters to make these into different shapes, and you can roll the dough thicker or thinner, as you prefer. As I said, the options for the flavourings you can add are almost limitless: milk (sweet), plain (semi-sweet) or white chocolate chips; your favourite chopped nuts; glacé (candied) cherries; chopped ready-to-eat dried apricots … the list goes on. You can also substitute grated lemon zest or ginger or other spices for the vanilla flavouring for even more options. At Christmas, I like to decorate the cookies with a little water icing (frosting); you could also pierce a hole in the top of the uncooked shapes with a skewer and thread them with a ribbon when cooked to hang on the Christmas tree.

Italian-style focaccia

Traditional Italian focaccia is simply the best, but it is full of olive oil. My version is not as oily, although you can make it moister by adding more olive oil before it is cooked or once it is out of the oven, when the oil will soak into the cooked dough.

SERVES 6–8

FOR THE FIRST YEAST MIXTURE
10 ml/2 tsp dried yeast

2.5 ml/½ tsp caster (superfine) sugar

250 ml/8 fl oz/1 cup warm water

175 g/6 oz/1½ cups plain
(all-purpose) flour

TO COMPLETE THE DOUGH
10 ml/2 tsp dried yeast

2.5 ml/½ tsp caster (superfine) sugar

250 ml/8 fl oz/1 cup warm water

90 ml/6 tbsp olive oil,
plus extra for pouring

5 ml/1 tsp sea salt,
plus extra for sprinkling

450 g/1 lb/4 cups plain
(all-purpose) flour

4 sprigs of fresh rosemary

4 sprigs of fresh thyme

1 To make the first yeast mixture, dissolve the yeast and sugar in a bowl with the warm water, then leave it to stand for 10 minutes until bubbles form on top.

2 Beat in the flour, cover and leave to stand in a warm place for about 1 hour until the mixture has risen.

3 To complete the dough, dissolve the yeast and sugar in a large bowl with the warm water, then leave it to stand for 10 minutes until the bubbles form on top.

4 Work in the olive oil and salt, then add the risen yeast mixture and beat together well. Gradually add enough of the flour a little at a time, beating with a wooden spoon, until you have a doughy consistency. Turn the dough out on to a floured work surface and knead in the rest of the flour. It will take about 10 minutes to knead the mixture to a soft, smooth dough.

5 Place the dough in an oiled bowl, cover with oiled clingfilm (plastic wrap) and leave in a warm place for about 1 hour to rise until it has doubled in size.

6 Knock back the dough by punching it and kneading it lightly. Lightly oil your hands to make handling the dough easier, then press it into flat rounds, either individual or large-sized. Transfer to greased baking (cookie) sheets, cover and leave to rise for 30 minutes.

7 Preheat the oven to 200°C/400°F/gas 6/fan oven 180°C.

8 Use your fingers to press dimples in the dough, then sprinkle on some sea salt and drizzle with olive oil. Break up the rosemary and thyme sprigs and sprinkle them over the focaccia.

9 Turn down the oven temperature to 180°C/350°F/gas 4/fan oven 160°C and bake the focaccia for 30–40 minutes until golden. Remove from the oven and sprinkle over some more olive oil, if liked, watching it soak into the bread.

10 Leave to cool slightly before serving whole or torn into pieces.

Serving suggestions This focaccia is delicious served with any dips (buy ready-made or see my recipes on pages 10–13) or as an accompaniment to any Italian-style main course.

Hints and variations If you have any focaccia left over, slit them in half and toast them for delicious snacks the next day.

To make a delicious grape focaccia, make a syrup with 225 g/ 8 oz/1 cup soft brown sugar and 120 ml/4 fl oz/½ cup sweet wine. Make the dough into two thin rounds and sandwich them together with half the syrup and 225 g/8 oz halved seedless grapes. Top with the remaining syrup and the same quantity of grapes and bake in a preheated oven at 180°C/350°F/gas 4/fan oven 160°C for 30 minutes until caramelised.

Mediterranean flavour Whenever I am cruising in Italy, I always buy fresh focaccia at local bread shops or delis. They often have them flavoured with olive, rosemary or onion, and some have cherry tomatoes in them too. Focaccia used to be something you could only enjoy on holiday, but you can now buy them at home in plenty of supermarkets and delicatessens.

Cinnamon stars

These are easy and quick but thoroughly delicious. As long as you keep some puff pastry in the freezer, you can always rustle them up when you have no time to prepare anything else.

MAKES ABOUT 30

250 g/9 oz/1 packet of puff pastry (paste)

1 egg yolk

15 ml/1 tbsp water

5 ml/1 tsp ground cinnamon

15 ml/1 tbsp icing (confectioners') sugar

1 Preheat the oven to 200°C/400°F/gas 6/fan oven 180°C and dampen a baking (cookie) sheet.

2 Roll out the pastry on a lightly floured surface to about 5 mm/¼ in thick. Using a star-shaped biscuit (cookie) cutter, cut the pastry into shapes and arrange them on the baking sheet.

3 Beat the egg yolk with the water and brush over the pastry.

4 Mix together the cinnamon and sugar and sprinkle half of the mixture over the top.

5 Bake in the oven for 15–20 minutes until risen and golden. Transfer to a wire rack, sprinkle with the remaining cinnamon sugar and leave to cool.

Serving suggestions These are delicious on their own, and if you're in a hurry they make a great dessert served with fruit salad or ice cream. For a special touch, I mix a little lemon and orange juice with a generous splash of vodka, pour it over some sliced fruits and leave it to macerate while I make the stars.

Hints and variations You can make these in any shape or size you like.

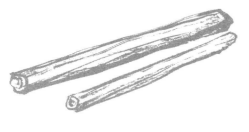